Lake Garda

www.marco-polo.com

How this Guide Works

Our guide introduces you to the sights at Lake Garda and its surroundings in four chapters. The map below presents an overview of how the chapters are arranged. Each one has been allocated a special colour. In order to help you plan your trip, we have subdivided all the main points of interest in each chapter into three sections: the must-see sights are listed under the *TOP 10* and also highlighted in the book with two stars. You'll find other important sites that didn't quite make our Top 10 list in the *Don't Miss* section. A selection of other places worth seeing appears in the *At Your Leisure* section.

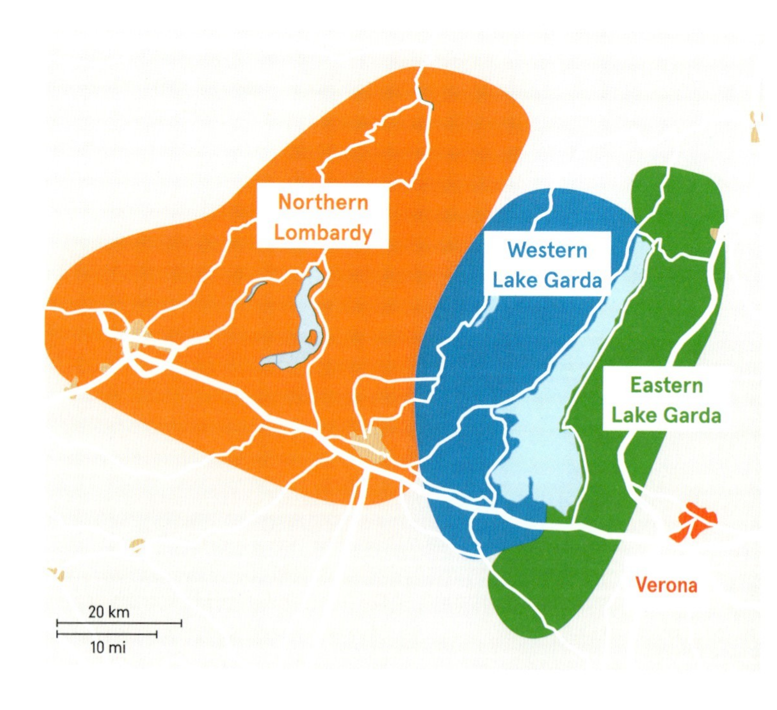

Practicalities

Walks & Tours

Appendix

Magical Moments

Be in the right place at the right time and experience magical moments you will never forget.

Your guarantee for spectacular views: Pieve di Tremosine on Lake Garda's northwestern shore.

Sightseeing from the water: the ferry 'Brennero' passes the Grand Hotel Gardone in Gardone Riviera

1

2

3

4

5

6

7

8

9

10

★★ TOP 10

Not to be missed! Our top hits – from the absolute No. 1 to No. 10 – help you plan your tour of the most important sights.

❶ ★★ Sirmione
Beautifully located on the south of the lake, Sirmione boasts one of the best preserved moated fortresses in Europe (p. 42)

❷ ★★ Malcesine & Monte Baldo
The 13th-century Castello Scaligero is one of the best-known landmarks on Lake Garda; Monte Baldo a place to escape the heat of summer down on the water (p. 74).

❸ ★★ Garda
With its wonderful lakeside promenade (Lungolago), Punta di San Vigilio around the corner and Isola del Garda a few minutes away by boat, the variety of attractions Lake Garda has to offer can all be enjoyed from just one place (p. 80).

❹ ★★ Salò
Reminders of the town's eventful history can be seen all down Lungolago, one of the most elegant promenades on the lake with a sophisticated atmosphere to match (p. 47).

❺ ★★ Riva del Garda
This little town became the haunt of poets, writers and philosophers at the turn of the 20th century. Its *grandezza* and beautiful architecture can still be seen today (p. 83).

❻ ★★ Piazza Bra & Arena di Verona
Who wouldn't want to sit on Verona's world-famous square, gazing at the Roman amphitheatre and dream of being Romeo or Juliet (p. 104)?

❼ ★★ Piazza dei Signori
Shakespeare may be better known but the memorial in the centre of Verona honours another great writer, the poet Dante Alighieri who wrote his masterpiece, the *Divine Comedy*, in this city (p. 108).

❽ ★★ Piazza delle Erbe
Verona's 'belly' – its market – provides a stage for everyday life set against a magnificent backdrop (p. 110).

❾ ★★ Bergamo
The *Città Alta* (Old Town) with the Piazza Vecchia is one of the most beautiful in northern Italy (p. 132).

❿ ★★ Lago d'Iseo
Framed by wooded slopes in the southern foothills of the Alps, Lago d'Iseo has the largest lake island in Central Europe – Monte Isola (p. 138),

That Lake Garda Feeling

Discover what makes Lake Garda as appealing as it is and experience its unique flair. Just as the locals do.

The first espresso after leaving the autostrada

Stop at the car park after the first hairpin bend coming from Nago heading for Torbole and enjoy your first cup of coffee, your first *aperol* or your first ice cream (at the bar on the other side of the road). The view to the south is breathtaking.

Racing through tunnels like James Bond

The first part of the Gardesana Occidentale that runs down the western side of the lake from Riva to Campione passes through at least a dozen tunnels which even inspired 007's motive scouts. Bond & Co. spent two weeks filming for *Quantum of Solace* on Lake Garda. That may only have resulted in a brief moment in the final film – but what a couple of minutes!

Trip on a paddle steamer

A trip across the lake on the 'Zanardelli' or the 'Italia' – two paddle steamers built in 1903 and 1908 respectively – is a must. The 'Zanardelli' operates in the north; the 'Italia' in the south. The locals love being out on the lake too, albeit generally in their own sailing boats. Alternatively you can hire a little motorboat with 40hp even if you don't have a driving licence.

Torbole at half-past-six: a bright and breezy spectacle

When the first rays of sunlight peak over Monte Baldo and the *pelèr*, the strong north wind, starts to pick up, you get the feeling that the whole of Torbole is out on a surfboard at the crack of dawn. The *lago* turns into a glimmering mass of butterfly-like forms. Colourful sails flatter over the water; the south starts to emerge and the new day begins with a bright and breezy spectacle: the windsurfing cracks are out on the water, speeding along or showing off their tricks. Distance fans race back and forth along a 2km (1¼mi) stretch between Torbole and Riva as if on a conveyor belt. Time and again. A fascinating sight to see.

Buona giornata! Claudio and Giacomo are ready to serve you your welcome drink and something to nibble in Torri del Benaco on the east side of Lake Garda.

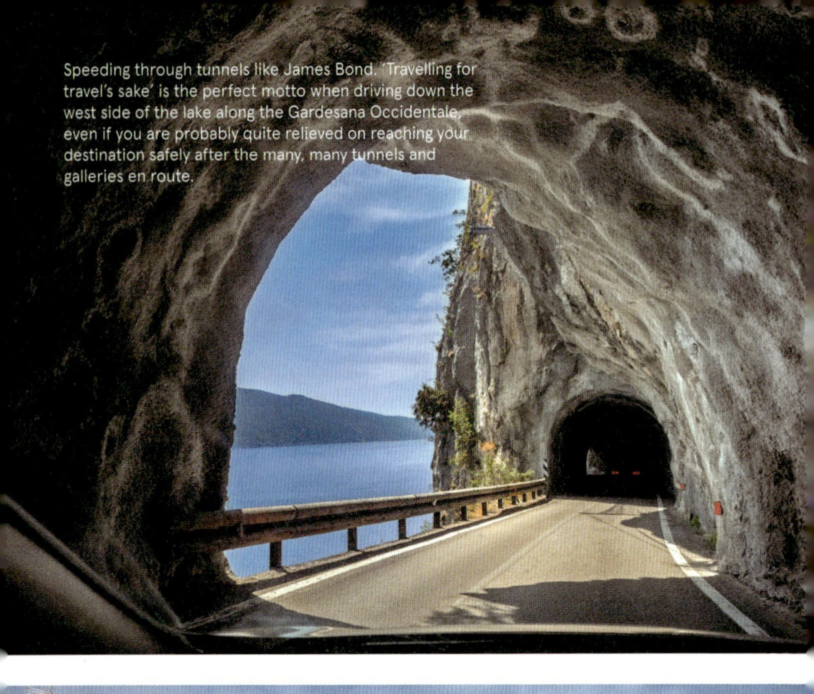

Speeding through tunnels like James Bond. 'Travelling for travel's sake' is the perfect motto when driving down the west side of the lake along the Gardesana Occidentale, even if you are probably quite relieved on reaching your destination safely after the many, many tunnels and galleries en route.

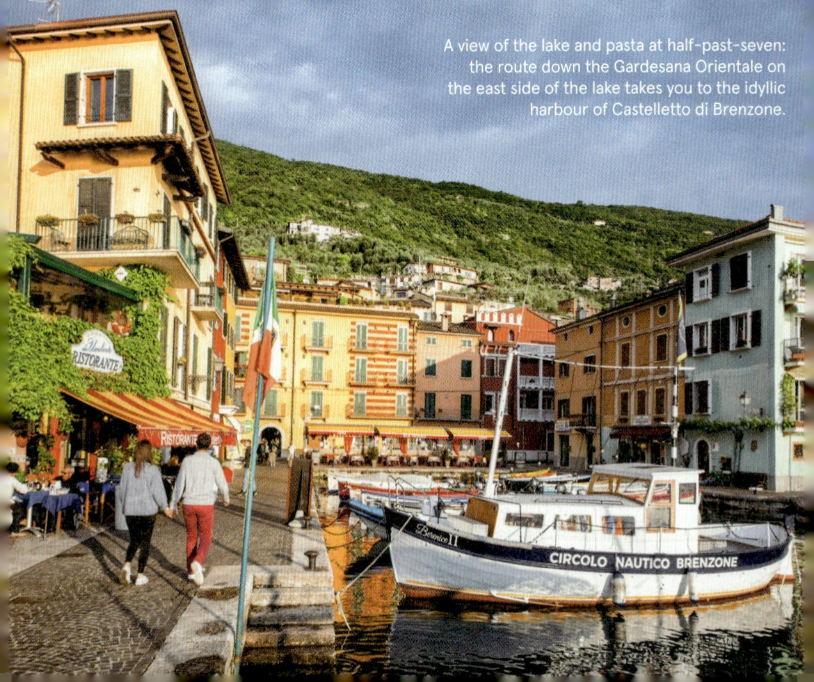

A view of the lake and pasta at half-past-seven: the route down the Gardesana Orientale on the east side of the lake takes you to the idyllic harbour of Castelletto di Brenzone.

A view of the lake and pasta at half-past-seven

In the evening, when the colour of the lake on the eastern shore changes from a brilliant silver to a soft gold in the light of the setting sun, sit back and enjoy an *aperol* or a 'Hugo' before your evening meal on the Gardesana Orientale at least once during your stay and watch the sun go down – either on a pontoon in Torri del Benaco or a balcony in the 'Belvedere' in Marniga di Brenzone, right on the water with a view of the castle in Malcesine on the Lido di Paina or in one of the small harbours like that at Castelletto di Brenzone.

Sunday evening on the beach

Lots of Italian families head for the lakeside in July and August even although it is often said that it is firmly in the hands of the Germans – which, considering the number of tourists who flood to the lake every year, is hardly surprising. However, when the Italians descend the situation changes noticeably. Tables, chairs and sun umbrellas appear early in the morning and air beds are pumped up. After a long, hot day, family get-togethers start at around half past seven in the evening with barbecues, *vino* and a huge variety of *antipasti*. And some of the fathers may have had a successful day's fishing. You may even be invited to a glass of something by your neighbours.

A magical and atmospheric evening

15 August, *Ferragosto,* is not only the highlight of the holiday season but also one of Italy's most important religious festivals. And Desenzano del Garda is the perfect place to mark this special holiday – with the 'notte d'incanto', the 'night of magic'. Thousands of little lights and candles float on the water. The lake glitters and sparkles like the eyes of those who take part. Just soak up the atmosphere.

A day in a deserted village

A 30-minute walk along a donkey track from Marniga di Brenzone will bring you to Campo. An artist has set up his easel, sheep are grazing nearby, a donkey is standing motionless in the blazing sun. Campo dates from the 11th century and is a quiet, solitary place albeit run down now. Hardly anyone lives here anymore as most people have moved away: no roads, no future – but a wonderful atmosphere.

A night in the Limonaia

The view of the bulbous lower end of the lake is simply stunning and the edge of the infinity pool merges optically with the water on Lake Garda 300m (985ft) below. You may be able to find a more exclusive place to stay in Lago, but nowhere is a beautiful as in 'Lefay' – the holiday resort above Gargnano (p. 56) that will give you that perfect 'lago' feeling.

The idyllic landscape at Punta di San Vigilio near Garda on the east side of the lake.

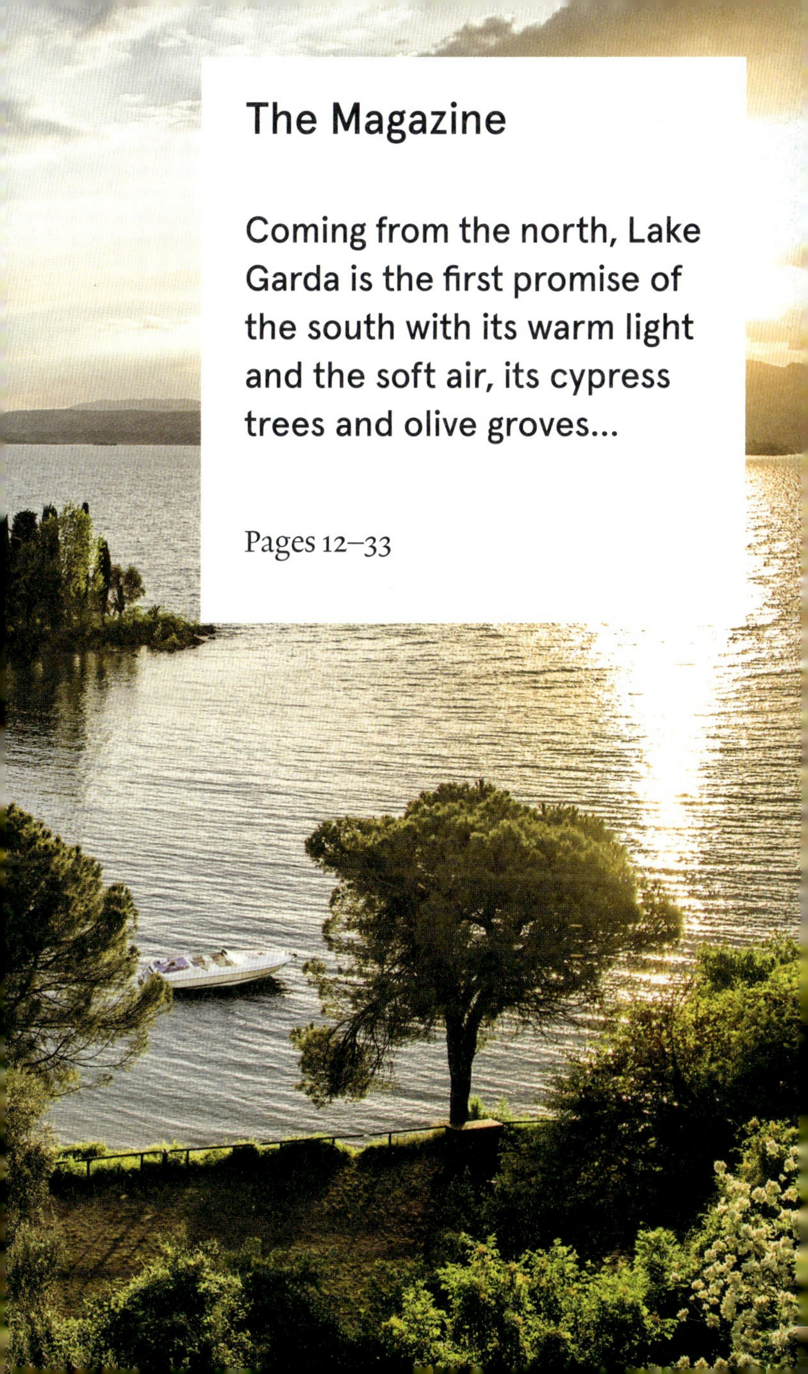

The Magazine

Coming from the north, Lake Garda is the first promise of the south with its warm light and the soft air, its cypress trees and olive groves…

Pages 12–33

Mountains, Rivers and Lakes

Everyone wants to be down on the *lago*. Even the Romans loved the lake and, since then, others have followed on their heels – from the rich and famous to the much less prominent. And that's still the case to this day. Its charm has stood the test of time and the majority of visitors return time and again. Why is that? Let's find out...

Sandwiched between the Alps to the north and the Apennines in the south is the Lombardy Plain. This low-lying, fertile region is bisected by the River Po. Italy's biggest river rises below Monte Viso – near Italy's western border with France – in Piedmont, named after its location at the 'foot of the mountains' (Latin: *ad pedem montium*). The river then flows eastwards, prevented from turning north or south by the mountain massifs and, on its way, it collects the water that flows out of the great lakes which define the geography of northern Italy.

Hiking from the Pregasina tunnel towards Riva, Lake Garda can be seen at its very best.

In the Cascata del Varone near Riva del Garda, the water has been gnawing into the rock for more than 20,000 years.

Carved by ice and snow

During the Pleistocene Ice Age, a period of about 1.5 million years, the movement of huge glaciers from the Alps followed the line of least resistance between ridges of harder rock. As they advanced the glaciers gouged out the valleys and ground the loose rock to a paste which was deposited as a moraine at the sides and head of the glacier. When the ice finally retreated, freshwater lakes, dammed by the moraine, formed in the extra deep valleys.

Fed from the north

This, Italy's largest lake with a surface area of around 370km² (230mi²), was known as Lacus Banacus in Antiquity after a Celtic deity. It owes its present name, Lago di Garda, to the eponymous town on the east side of the lake. With a depth of up to 346m (1135ft), the *lago* is fed mainly by the Sarca, a river that flows into the lake in the north near Torbole and flows out again in the south – as the Mincio – near Peschiera del Garda.

Fertile shores

Lake Garda's fertile shores and the abundance of freshwater fish have attracted human settlers since time immemorial. The wide band of rich soil around the edge of the lake was formed by the magnesium-rich limestone brought down as a glacial moraine from the Brenta Dolomites to the north. On the northern shore the strip of fertile moraine is much narrower. In places on the western side the high ridge descends directly into the lake. On this shore agriculture was more difficult, although more concentrated crops flourished – olives and vines on the eastern side, lemons on the west. Today the vines are still there, growing grapes for Bardolino wines. Olive trees continue to flourish here too, giving the eastern shore its name – the Olive Riviera, now renowned for its excellent olive oil. Only a few *limonaie* growing lemon trees, however, are to be found on the western coast today.

History, Fact & Fiction

From the prehistoric pile dwellings of the first settlers on the lake to the arrival of the first tourists in the 19th century, the history of Lake Garda and the surrounding area includes many interesting facts. One of these is about the founding of the Red Cross.

In 1842 a Turin newspaper, *Il Risorgimento* (The Awakening), alerted Italians to the fact that their country, once the heart of the Roman Empire, was now ruled by foreigners. Spain controlled much of the south, Austria much of the north, while the rest of Italy was in the hands of small factional states. Spurred on by the newspaper, Italians yearned for the unification of their country but this was to take many years and cost many lives – a great number of those being lost in two major battles fought in 1859 close to Lake Garda's southern shore.

On 4 June the French defeated the Austrian army at Magenta. The Austrians retreated towards the stronghold they had created around Peschiera del Garda and on 24 June at Solferino, to the south of Sirmione, they lay in wait. Emperor Franz Josef himself led the army: against him were the French under Napoleon I and the Piedmont troops under Vittorio Emanuele I – three crowned heads together on one battlefield. As dawn broke the French attacked the main Austrian force, while the Italians attacked the Austrian right-wing to the south at San Martino, a total of 270,000 men fighting.

Man to man

The tide of this second battle ebbed and flowed for about 15 hours, the stamina of the soldiers being remarkable. But weaponry had improved since the last great land battle in Europe and the carnage was appalling. Some estimates of are 40,000 men dying that day, and all agree that losses exceeded 25,000 men. As night approached the Austrians retreated behind their defences at Peschiera, allowing the French and Italians to claim victory, although it is probable that they had actually lost more men. The suffering of the injured was terrible. In the heat of the Italian summer many lay for hours as the battle continued around them. Then a violent storm soaked those who had somehow survived. Their suffering led the Swiss businessman and humanist Henri Dunant to found the Red Cross as, faced by such a reality, he realised that "Civilisation means providing mutual help, man to man, nation to nation."

Napoleon was so appalled by the destruction that he immediately proposed a peace plan to Franz Josef, the Austrian Emperor. In a treaty signed at Villafranca, now the site of Verona's airport, he secured Lombardy for the 'new' Italy, but left the Austrians in Veneto, much to the disgust and dismay of the people of Piedmont. It was to be another seven years of fighting before Veneto finally fell to Italy.

Wanted territory

Though Solferino was the bloodiest battle fought near the lakes, it was

The Museo di Sant Giulia in Brescia traces the history of the Lombards. Their former seat of power in Italy has since become a UNESCO World Heritage site. Highlights of the collection include the 'Winged Victoria' (below, left), a bronze statue almost two metres high, dating from the second quarter of the 1st century, and the gem-studded 'Desiderius' cross (9th century, below). The latter stands under a cross vault decorated with stars taken from the medieval church of Santa Maria in Solario (left).

not the only one. Probably the most incredible took place in the early 15th century when the Milanese army marched east to besiege Brescia, a Venetian outpost. Unable to relieve the siege by land, the Venetians attempted to do so by water. A fleet of galleys, some of them war ships, others supply vessels, was dismantled in Venice, loaded onto ox carts and towed to the River Adige. There the 26 galleys were rebuilt, launched and rowed upstream to Rovereto where they were again dismantled. From here 2,000 oxen were used to haul them to northern Lake Garda over the San Giovanni Pass. It took three months to get the ships to the lake. By then, things were desperate in Brescia and the ships were hastily rebuilt. Although barely serviceable, they were launched and sailed south. At Maderno they were met by a Milanese fleet and defeated. The battle was lost. However, in the end, Venice ultimately won the war.

Timeline

4000BC Early Bronze Age settlers living around Brescia.

1000BC Celts and Etruscans move into the area.

300BC The Romans defeat the Gaulish Cisalpine empire and the lakes area becomes part of the Roman Empire. The Roman remains at Sirmione, Desenzano and Brescia are among the finest in northern Italy. Verona's amphitheatre (above) is one of the best examples of its kind outside Rome.

5th century AD The western Roman empire falls and the Lombards settle what is now Lombardy. Queen Theodolinda of the Lombards converts to Christianity and makes it the 'state' religion. For her services to the faith the Pope gives Theodolinda a True Nail – one of the nails used in the Crucifixion. It is incorporated into the Iron Crown used at the coronation of the Italian kings and is now in Monza Cathedral.

8th century Charlemagne defeats the Lombards and a

Carolingian kingdom is established across the lakes area.
9th/10th centuries Carolingian rule ends. The Lombards retake the area but are replaced first by the Magyars, then by the Saxons.
12th–15th centuries Era of the city states. The della Scala (Scaligeri) family hold Verona and Lake Garda, eventually being replaced by the Venetians. To the west the Viscontis and Sforzas of Milan take control.
16th century The Venetians hold Lake Garda, but the land to the west is controlled by the Spanish.
18th century The War of the Spanish Succession (1700–14) ends with Austria controlling Lake Garda and Savoy holding the western lakes. Napoleon frees northern Italy, but Austrian rule is then reimposed.
19th century *Il Risorgimento* unites all Italians in a desire for an Italian state. At a decisive battle in 1859 at Solferino the Austrians are defeated. Finally, in 1870 Italy is unified under King Vittorio Emanuele I.
20th century The Treaty of St Germain cedes Trentino to Italy in 1919. Mussolini signs the 'Pact of Steel' with Hitler (1939), then takes Italy into a war for which she is ill prepared.
In 1943 Mussolini falls from power. Hitler creates the Salò Republic (below: the town's lakeside promenade) on Lake Garda as the new Italian government declares war on Germany.
Partisans execute Mussolini in 1945. The following year King Vittorio Emanuele I abdicates and Italy becomes a republic. The Treaty of Rome in 1957 creates the European Common Market which later evolves into the EU.
21st century The populist centre-right politician and long-standing Prime Minister (1994/1995, 2001–2006, 2008–2011) Silvio Berlusconi is convicted of tax fraud in 2014. In just seven years, from 2011 until 2018, five different prime ministers have held this office: Mario Monti, Enrico Letta, Matteo Renzi, Paolo Gentiloni and Giuseppe Conte.

Fauna and Flora

A wide variety of Mediterranean and sub-tropical plants flourish in the mild climate of the Lake Garda region that is also a rich farming region for fruit and olives, well-known for its wines.

The much-heralded garden and park-like landscape around Lake Garda has little to do with untouched nature as it is much more a cultivated area of fruit trees and vineyards, fig and citrus plantations and olive groves. The once widely spread forests of evergreen holm oaks have now been severely decimated. Ancient beechwoods, however, can still be found today near Prada on Monte Baldo. The evergreen laurel is much more common; the Judas tree on the other hand increasingly rare. Sweet chestnuts ripen at high altitudes. The mulberry bushes were originally planted for silkworm farms.

Cypresses and cedars of Lebanon, as well as palm trees and agaves, set picturesque accents along the lake shore. Lime trees and maples have been planted to create avenues. Azaleas, oleander bushes, magnolias and acacias fill the air with their scent in the spring and summer. Reed

Grapes grow very well in the vineyards in the northwest corner of Lake Garda, too.

The south in full bloom: in the garden at the Town Hall of Limone on the west side of the lake

beds and rushes, kingcups, water lilies and water clover can be found in the few flat and marshy areas along the banks of the lake.

The Corna Piana di Brentonico nature reserve on Monte Baldo lies at an altitude of between 1276m (4186ft) and 1735m (5692ft). Preglacial plants have survived, including cobweb saxifrage *(Saxifraga arachnoidea)*, sticky columbine *(Aquilegia thalictrifolia)* and the Dolomite tufted horned rampion *(Physoplexis comosa)*. Endemic plants are the long-stemmed Monte Baldo anemone *(Anemone baldensis)*, South Tyrol cleaver *(Galium baldensis)* and the white-haired Monte Baldo sedge *(Carex baldensis)*.

The Monte Baldo truffle is much-loved by gourmands. The same is true for the lemons, the olives – from which the best olive oil is produced – and the grapes for the excellent wines.

Red and fallow deer, as well as chamois, have now returned to the Parco Alto Garda Bresciano. The Monte Baldo nature reserve is also home to the capercaillie, the rock partridge, the lynx, the hare, the fox and martens. The fauna of Monte Baldo also includes poisonous snakes, although they are very rare, and scorpions that can be seen more frequently in May and September in particular. All sorts of different lizards bathe on the warm walls of buildings and, every now and again, you may come across a slowworm. The variety of butterflies is impressive; they find sufficient nourishment from the many flowers that grow in the Monte Baldo region.

A number of different species of duck, coot and heron have settled in the nature park along the Oglio and Mincio rivers. Seagulls have adapted themselves well to the living conditions on Lake Garda and eagles and falcons can be watched every now and again as they soar majestically above the slopes.

Non-venemous snakes live in a few places on the water's edge and, near beaches, may be seen peeking out of the water, especially in August, or making a quick dash to hide under the nearest stone. In the water itself, Garda lake trout and Garda lake carp can reach an impressive size. Char, eel, tench, perch, pike and barbel are becoming increasingly rare.

Culinary Delights

The essence of the Italian diet is simplicity – high-quality ingredients prepared with the minimum of fuss. Sauces and dressings are, in general, kept to a minimum, with the cooking allowing the ingredients to speak for themselves.

The basis of many meals is, of course, pasta, but there is also a surprising amount of rice eaten as there are extensive rice fields close to Padua, south of Milan, and near Venice. The best known rice dishes are *risotto alla milanese*, rice with saffron, and *risotto alla monzese,* with minced meat and tomato added. Mantova also has a risotto speciality, a rich mix of rice, butter and onions, while a popular form in the Veneto region is *risotto nero*, rice coloured (and flavoured) with squid ink.

Pasta comes in a bewildering variety of forms, each with its own name. The array of shapes seems over-the-top – surely, if they are all made from the same ingredients, they must taste the same? But no, they don't – although the differences are subtle. Basically, there are two types of pasta made either of flour and water or flour and egg. (*pasta all'uovo*). Whatever the pasta, there will be a sauce, the most popular being *al pomodoro*, with tomatoes, *alla carbonara*, with bacon or ham and eggs, *alle vongole*, with clams, *alla bolognese*, with minced meat, herbs and vegetables and *con aglio, olio e peperoncino* (with garlic, olive oil and spicy pepperoni.

As a change from pasta and rice you could try polenta, a maize-based dish often served as an accompaniment to meat, as well as an antipasto. There is also gnocchi, made from chestnut flour and mashed potato.

Pizzerias can be found in every town and village. The most popular types of pizza are the simple *margharitta* (with tomato sauce and cheese) and *quattro formaggi*, which often uses local varieties of cheese.

Starters

Local antipasti include *bresaola*, thin-sliced, air-dried, salted beef,

Whether at or in the lake: having fun on Lago di Garda is a just a question of the mood you're in.

and *missoltini*, sun-dried fish, often eaten with a drop of vinegar and served with oil and a little polenta.

First course

Primi include pasta dishes, such as spaghetti, ravioli – a rich ravioli of cheese and butter is a speciality of the Bergamo area; the best tortellini comes from Valeggio sul Mincio, to the south of the lake – lasagne or minestrone soup, sometimes so thick with vegetables that, with bread, it is a meal in itself.

Main course

It is no surprise to find fish from the lake on most menus as a *secondo*. There are many types of fish, but the most popular are perch – delicious when fried lightly in olive oil – and fried trout. Around Lake Garda look out for *salmo carpio*, a trout only

Some of the best ice cream on Lake Garda can be found at the Gelateria Cristallo in Bardolino.

found in this area. One typical way of serving it is *in carpione*: the fish is fried or grilled and then left in a spicy vinegar/wine marinade for several hours. The dish is served cold. This method dates from the time when refrigerators were unknown and enables fish to be kept longer.

Veal (*vitello*) is a favourite meat dish and can be served in wine (*cotoletta al vino bianco*), with lemon (*al limone*) or a *cotoletta alla milanese*, a wafer-thin variation of the Viennese Schnitzel.

Grilled dishes, including beef (*manzo*), pork (*maiale*) and lamb (*agnello*), can be found on most menus. On Lago di Orta and in Mantua, in particular, but also in Verona, donkey meat – *asino* – is often used as the basis for a variety of different stews and hotpots.

Desserts

The Italians may not have invented it, but they are considered the best ice-cream makers in the world. If you want something more substantial as a dessert, try the *amaretti* (macaroons) or *millefoglie* at 'Perbellini' in Verona – a heavenly flaky-pastry creation.

On top of these there is always *pannacotta* and all sorts of pastries and cakes. The famous Milanese dessert *panettone*, a buttery cake with sultanas and succade, can always be found on the shelves around Christmas time.

And to drink

Italian wine is graded either DS (*Denominazione Semplice*), with no quality standard, DOC (*Denominazione di Origine Controllata*) or DOCG (*Denominazione di Origine Controllata e Garantita*), the highest standard.

The Franciacorta area around Lake Iseo produces good red wine and a delicious, sparkling white. But the most famous wines from the lakes area are those from Lake Garda's eastern shore: the light dry red Bardolino, the more full-bodied reds of the Valpolicella and the dry white Soave.

The fruity, dry white wine, Lugana, is produced on the south shore of the lake; the heavy red Gropello in the Valtènesi region to the southwest.

After the meal, perhaps a coffee. Cappucino, locally called *cappucio*, is usually served only at breakfast. The traditional coffee is *liscio*, black and strong, and served in a very small cup. The Italians add lots of sugar. There is also *ristretto*, which is even stronger. To tone either down try *lungo*, with hot water, *macchiato,* with a little milk, or *Americano*, the familiar coffee with milk seen throughout Europe.

The alternative to coffee is hot chocolate (*cioccolata calda*). The normal form is so thick that a spoon will stand up in it. Tea (*tè*) is not the Italians' strong point.

Italian firewater

Grappa, a traditional Italian spirit, comes from Lake Garda, predominantly from around Trentino. It is made from the pressed skins of grapes left over after winemaking. The liquid is fermented, without adding sugar, then distilled into a clear, dry spirit of between 80 and 90 proof. The strength of the grappa depends on the type of grape used. For lovers of that special taste, grappa is also available in a variety of different flavours with herbs, berries or dried roots, for example. Excellent liquors, made with fruit such as apricots or pears, can also be found. Of distilled drinks, those from Lake Como's Abbazia di Piona are the most famous. *Gocce Imperiali* (Imperial Drops), a herb-based spirit, is a potent monastical brew. On Lake Garda, *Acqua di cedro*, distilled in Salò, is a brandy made with citron.

Art & Culture

From Antiquity to the modern day. The region's architectural highlight is certainly the magnificent amphitheatre in Verona. However, many of the castles and beautiful churches and the traditional villas built along the shore of Lake Garda in the 19th century, are equally interesting. And when talking about art and culture, music – of course – plays a very big role in Italy.

The area around Lake Garda is blessed with a wealth of attractions. In addition to its natural beauty, it boasts a multitude of sights that not only testify to its rich artistic and cultural past but also to the present day, too. The Museo di Arte Moderna e Contemporanea di Trento e Rovereto (MART) in Rovereto, for instance, is considered one of the most important European institutes for modern and contemporary art. Churches and museums wait to be explored as well as public spaces

A masterpiece of Romanesque architecture: the main portal of the cathedral of Santa Maria Matricolare in Verona

An Overview

Pre-history (4000BC–1000BC)

On Isola Virginia, an island in Lake Varese (a small lake near the town of Varese, towards Lake Maggiore) there are remains from Neolithic to Bronze Age times. The Ledro lake dwellings (right) also date from the Bronze Age.

Roman (753BC–5th c.)

The Romans developed the 'classical' form of architecture of the Greeks. Verona's Arena is one of the finest Roman ruins in Europe. Domestic architecture, typical of that period, can be seen in the Villa Romana at Desenzano del Garda, while the villa at Sirmione (Grotte di Catullo) is one of the largest and most palatial ever found.

Lombard (6th–8th c.)

A Lombard church that has been excavated in the area behind the high altar in San Severo in Lazise is one of the few relics from this period. Beautiful works of Lombard art can be seen in the Museo di Santa Giulia in Brescia (p. 145). The medieval church of San Salvatore, the Romanesque church of Santa Maria of Solario and Santa Giulia from the 16th century have all been incorporated into today's museum complex.

Carolingian (8th–9th c.)

The church of San Zeno at Bardolino dates in part from the 8th century. One of the oldest churches in Italy, it is among the few survivors from the Carolingian era as later builders often demolished early churches and used the stone for their own buildings.

Romanesque (10th–12th c.)

The Romanesque style evolved from an amalgamation of Classical and Oriental influences. A Romanesque church façade has a tall, central section with the main entrance, rising to a pointed triangle at the top. To each side there are lower, symmetrical sections with sloping roofs. One of the best examples is the church of San Zeno Maggiore in Verona. The cathedral in Cremona is also very typical of this style.

Gothic (13th–14th c.)

The flamboyant architecture of the Gothic period was begun by Cistercian monks and rapidly taken up by other orders, and then by the builders of town churches. One of the most important architects was Arnolfo di Cambio. His signature style can be seen in Salò's *duomo* (cathedral).

Renaissance (15th–16th c.)

The Renaissance saw a return to the symmetry and beautiful proportions of Classical architecture. Palladio's Vicenza is as far as you need to travel to see the best of Renaissance architecture.

Baroque (17th–18th c.)

The Baroque style, with its flamboyant swirls and scrolls, was a reaction to the austerity of the Reformation. The façade of Bergamo's *duomo* is a good example.

Neoclassical (19th c.)

Once again, this style draws on the classical ideals of Antiquity and, in the area around Venice, is often a reference to the architectural works of Palladio. One example of the interior of the Duomo San Martino in Peschiera del Garda.

Art Nouveau (early 20th c.)

There is no better place to look than the villas built by Giuseppe Sommaruga at Sarnico on Lake Iseo.

20th/21st century

In the early 20th century, Functionalism, also known as the International Style, emerged as a prevalent answer to the decorative architectural styles of previous eras. The fundamental architectural principle behind this was that it should be possible to deduce a building's function from its appearance. As a contrast to this, the architectural style of the fascist state in Italy had a Neo-Classicist, Imperial Roman leaning.

It was not until after World War II that modern architecture found a foothold. The Venetian Carlo Scarpa (1906–78) addressed the subject of 'critical restoration' *(restauro critico)*; Pier Luigi Nervi (1891–1979) of Sondrio was one of the most important proponents of the use of reinforced concrete. The Museo d'Arte Moderna e Contemporanea di Trento e Rovereto in Rovereto (2002), considered one of the most important buildings of the modern day, was designed by the star architect Mario Botta from the canton of Ticino in Switzerland.

Drawing on the ideals of Antiquitiy: Palladio's Villa Rotonda nar Vicenza.

An opera being perfomed in the Arena di Verona: "Music gives a soul to the universe, wings to the mind, flight to the imagination and life to everything." (Plato)

where both traditional and current movements in art can be experienced at the most varied of celebrations and festivals around the lake. Music has always been immensely important and, today, ranges from the Pasqua Musicale Arcense held annually in Arco to the Vittoriale summer concert in Gardone and the Verona Opera Festival.

Viva la musica

Having given the world the violin it is no surprise that the lakes area – around Lake Garda in particular – has a strong musical tradition.

Gasparo de Salò (born at Salò on Lake Garda in 1540) and Andrea Amati of Cremona (c. 1520–80) each have, in their own way, a claim to how the modern violin evolved. Few people, however, will disagree that Antonio Stradivarius (c. 1644–1737), also from Cremona, was the finest violin-maker of them all. The secret of Stradivarius' manufacturing techniques is still debated. It is known that he scoured forests for the perfect tree. He used maple and spruce for the body of his instruments, pear and willow for the neck, but his drying techniques and the ingredients of his varnish are still unknown.

The region has also produced some famous composers: Luca Morenzio (c. 1553–1599) who was born near Brescia, Claudio Monteverdi (1567–1643) from Cremona and Gaetano Donizetti (1797–1848) born in Bergamo. Mention must also be made of Giuseppe Verdi (1813–1901) for, although he was not born in the area, he set Rigoletto close to Mantova.

Sport is (Not Just) in the Air

Lake Garda is a paradise not only for surfers and sailing enthusiasts, but also for cyclists, mountain bikers, hikers and climbers.

Where else can sport be so fascinating and such an intense experience other than in the breathtaking scenery around Lake Garda?

Swimming, sailing, diving

Thanks to its lovely bays, Lake Garda has long been a popular destination for northern Europeans looking for somewhere to swim or to enjoy water sports. There are free beaches (*spiaggia*) and bathing areas (*lido*), where you have to pay, all around the lake. As most of the beaches are pebbly, flip-flops are highly recommended. Every year water samples are taken from 65 beaches around the lake and tested by the regional authority for the protection of the environment. Approval has officially been given for swimming everywhere on the lake. Up-to-date data on the quality of the water can be called up under www.arpa.veneto.it or www.ats-brescia.it.

Lake Garda is also a favourite for sailing enthusiasts. There are some two dozen sailing clubs around the

Whether windsurfing or kitesurfing – Lake Garda always has something for everyone

Hikers (above: on the trail from the Pregasina Tunnel to Riva), climber (top left: on a high-rope course not far from Torbole) and cyclists (left: Monte Baldo): all enjoy perfect conditions for their sport on and near Lake Garda.

lake which also welcome guests. There are some good sites for hobby divers – especially off Riva (north shore), Salò (west shore) and Torri del Benaco (east shore), as well as Peschiera and Desenzano (both on the south shore).

Windsurfing & co.

On Lake Garda, starting before dawn, the *pelèr* (or *suer*) blows from the north. This lasts until around lunchtime when there is a period of relative calm before the *ora* begins to blow around 2 pm from the south, continuing through the afternoon and evening. Such dependable winds are a gift from the gods to anyone wishing to sail or windsurf. The winds are at their best at the northern end of the lake where it narrows and, thanks to the height of the mountain ridges all around, the air is funnelled making conditions even more favourable. For water skiers the situation is more difficult, as the use of power boats is restricted, particularly near popular bathing and windsurfing areas. A completely new water-sport that celebrated its world premiere a few years ago in Brenzone manages without either the wind or waves: an electric surfboard that reaches speeds of up to 25km/h (15mph).

JP
NEILPRYDE
RYDE HD
NEILPRYDE
JP

Hiking...

Monte Baldo is the best-known hiking area on Lake Garda and hikers are so spoilt by its natural beauty and variety that many people do not just come here once but return time and again. Three peaks, including the 2218m (7277ft)-high Cima Valdritta, accentuate the massif that stretches over a length of 40km (25mi). Its rocky face drops abruptly to the lake to the west whereas,. The summit can be reached from Malcesine in the comfort of a cablecar. There are a number of different paths for walkers across the extensive plateau. The Sentiero del Ventrar, a two-hour circular tour starting from the upper terminus, is popular. It is however only for experienced walkers with a head for heights. Cables have been mounted for greater safety at exposed sections. The views over Lake Garda and Malcesine are breathtaking. On the opposite side of the lake, the Parco Alto Garda Bresciano boasts a wide range of hiking trails. In the Valle delle Cartiere easy paths take you along the banks of the bubbling trout stream from Toscolano Maderno to the ruins of several old paper mills.

More challenging is the six-hour circular hike from Pregàsina which takes you across Cima della Nara and Cima al Bal. Time and again fantastic views of Lago di Garda – and of its little brother, Lago di Ledro – open up. The passage between the mountain pastures bursting with wild flowers on Prati di Guil and the craggy ridge that links the two peaks is breathtakingly beautiful, but the path is narrow and exposed.

A child-friendly hike follows the Old Ponale Road from the Ledro valley to Lake Garda. The path winds its way down towards Lake Garda, dropping 300m (985ft) through a series of steep hairpin bends. To the left, the cliff face rises up almost vertically; to the right it drops down just as steeply to the lake below. Riva is reached after about 2½ hours.

Climbing

Arco, in the very north of Lake Garda, is a mecca for free-climbers and where the international championships are held every year.

Cycling

There is also a wide spectrum of alternatives open to cycling enthusiasts too. These range from gentle bike tours on level terrain to trips along the shore of the lake and demanding mountain routes. Attractive mountain trails for cyclists can be found to the north of Lake Garda. The Parco Alto Garda Bresciano mentioned above is a paradise for mountain bikers.

In Torbole a shuttle service is provided to take you to the top.

Between the sky and the lake: Tremosine has a spectacular setting, some 350m above the lake, in the northern section of the west shore.

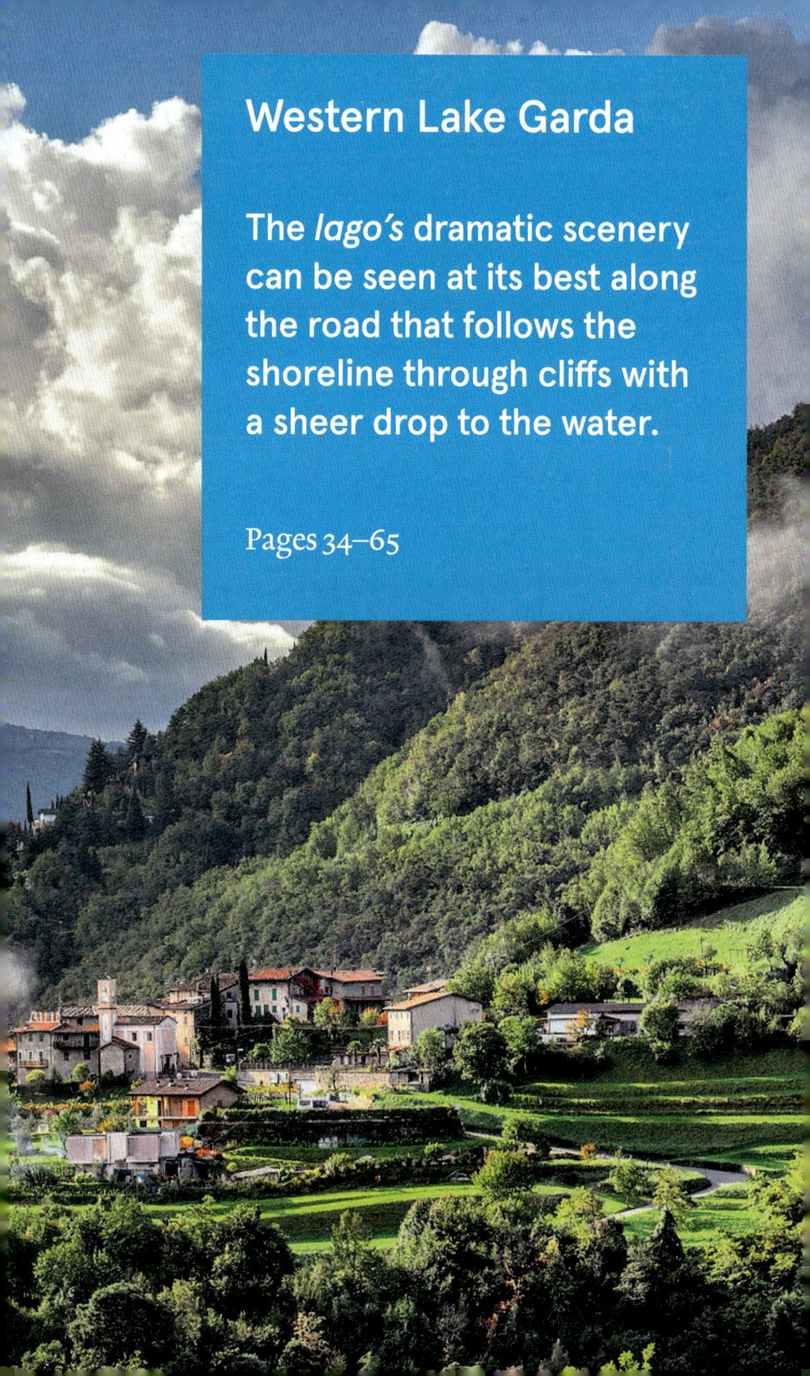

Western Lake Garda

The *lago's* dramatic scenery can be seen at its best along the road that follows the shoreline through cliffs with a sheer drop to the water.

Pages 34–65

Getting Your Bearings

The west shore of Lake Garda is often referred to as the 'Lemon coast' – referring to the first citrus plantation on the lake in the former fishing village of Limone. This was the shore where big villas were built, despite the fact that the terrace between the foot of the rising mountains and the water's edge is narrower here.

The famous *Gardesana Occidentale* – for which 74 tunnels were blasted through the rock – leads down the western side of the lake from Riva del Garda in the far north to Salò in the south. Virtually everywhere sheer cliff faces stretch up towards the sky. Nevertheless, there are several lovely places along the route and on the slopes above that all exude a charm of their very own. Among sites worth seeing are magnificent estates such as Vittoriale degli Italiani created by the eccentric writer Gabriele d'Annunzio in Gardone that also boasts another attraction, the Botanic Garden at the Fondazione André Heller. Salò, that adjoins immediately to the south, is the largest town on the west side of the lake. High above Limone and Gardone are the twin plateaus of Tignale and Tremosine. This is a quiet rural area offering spectacular views.

TOP 10

❶ ★★ Sirmione
❹ ★★ Salò

Don't Miss

⓫ Gardone Riviera

At Your Leisure

12 Lago di Ledro
13 Limone sul Garda
14 Tremosine & Tignale
15 Gargnano
16 Villa & Bogliaco
17 Lago di Valvestino
18 Lago d'Idro
19 Toscolano-Maderno
20 Isola del Garda
21 Desenzano del Garda

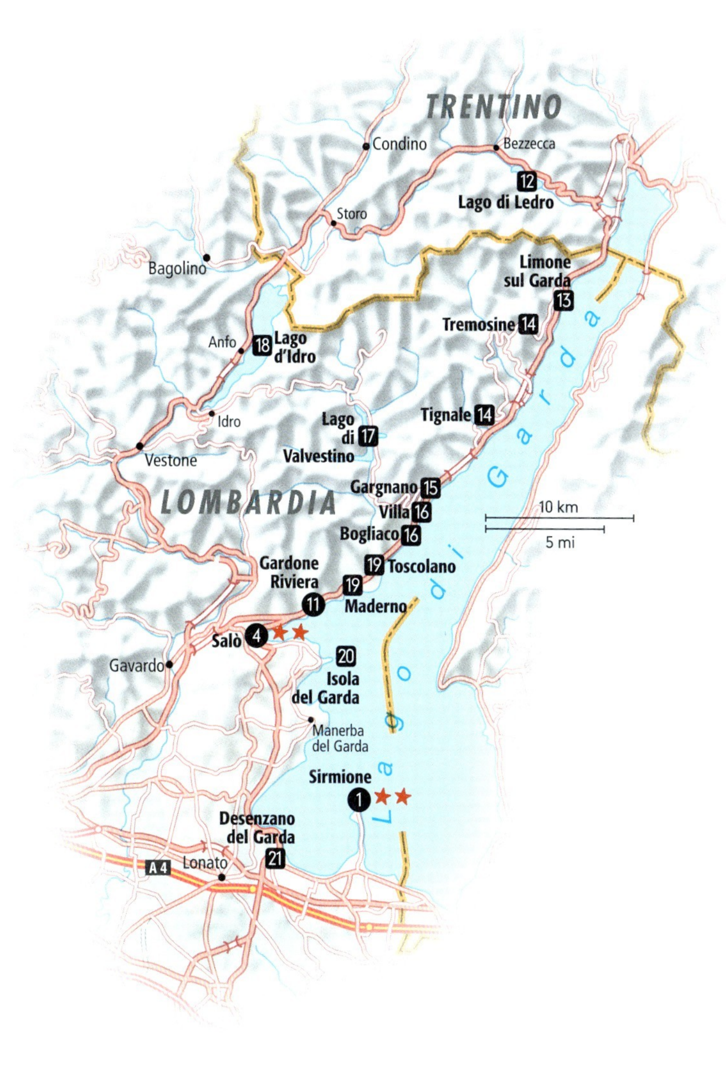

TRENTINO
Condino
Bezzecca
12
Lago di Ledro
Storo
Bagolino
Limone
sul Garda
13
Tremosine 14
Anfo
18 Lago
d'Idro
Idro
Lago
di 17
Valvestino
Tignale 14
Vestone
LOMBARDIA
Gargnano 15
Villa 16
Bogliaco 16
10 km
5 mi
Gardone
Riviera
19 Toscolano
19
11
Maderno
Salò 4
Gavardo
20
Isola
del Garda
Manerba
del Garda
Sirmione
1
Lago di Garda
Desenzano
del Garda
21
A 4
Lonato

My Day of Nostalgia and Grandezza

The German Emperor Wilhelm I, the Austrian Empress Elisabeth and King Farouk of Egypt all visited Lake Garda around 1900 when health resorts attracted those seeking the winter sun and tourism on the lake first started. Let's have a look (and experience) how much of that grandezza of old has survived to this day.

10am: Head for the island

A lovely morning in ❹ ★★ Salò: across the water is the 20 Isola del Garda, arguably the most beautiful spot on the lake – a paradise of flowers, architecture and peace. See for yourself (April–Oct., www.isoladelgarda.com)!

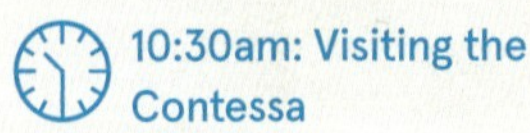

10:30am: Visiting the Contessa

The crossing by boat takes around 15 minutes and Contessa Alberta is there to greet us at the *piccolo porto* on the island. She is wearing a pink top, a denim skirt, flip-flops and has a tattoo. That matches her friendly welcome: "Please don't call me *contessa!*" she says. "My name is Alberta and I'll be showing you around the Isola del Garda". She is one of the island's eight owners – together with her mother and six brothers and sisters. Charlotte Chetwynd-Talbot, her mother, an English aristocrat, fell in love with a dashing *ragazzo* when visiting Rome without knowing who he was. Camillo Cavazza, at that time, was the sole owner of the *isola*. Since Camillo Cavazza's death in 1981,

7:30pm: A two-starred finale
End
7:30pm
Villa Feltrinelli
15
Villa Bogliaco
7pm
6:30pm
6:30pm: The Palace-on-the-Lake
7pm: Promenading along the lakeside
3pm: Somewhere between lunacy and genius
1:30pm: Luncheon at the Casino
2 km
1 mi
Toscolano Maderno
Lago di Garda
1:30 pm
3pm
Il Vittoriale degli Italiani
Ristorante Casino
Villa Florida
5:30pm
Grand Hotel Fasano
11
Grand Hotel Gardone
Start
5:30pm: Music at tea-time
10am
4
1pm
20
10:30am
1pm: Violin music in the air
10:30am: Visiting the Contessa

The countess' home: palatial splendour on Isola del Garda.

Charlotte, her seven children and their families have continued to live on the island. Alberta's apartment is in the beautiful tower.

1pm: Violin music in the air

Back in ❹ ★★ Salò again, the little town has a lot to offer: history, art and well-known people such as Gasparo da Salò who – together with Andrea Amati and Antonio Stradivari – is considered one of the first and most famous violin makers. There is a monument to Gasparo at the beginning of the lakeside promenade.

1:30pm: Luncheon at the Casino

Feeling hungry? For a late lunch go on to ⓫ Gardone Riviera. The Ristorante Casino dates back to 1909 and still has probably the most authentic Belle Époque atmosphere anywhere on Lake Garda. Its location with a terrace above the water is breathtaking and the food delicious!

3pm: Somewhere between lunacy and genius

Vittoriale degli Italiani lies a little above Gardone. It is a strange mixture of art and kitsch, *grandezza* and petite bourgeoisie. You should plan 2 hours for a look around Gabriele d'Annunzio's temple, a potpourri, comprising a large portion of poetic fantasy, lots of dandy ingenuity and a barely comprehensible passion for all things military...

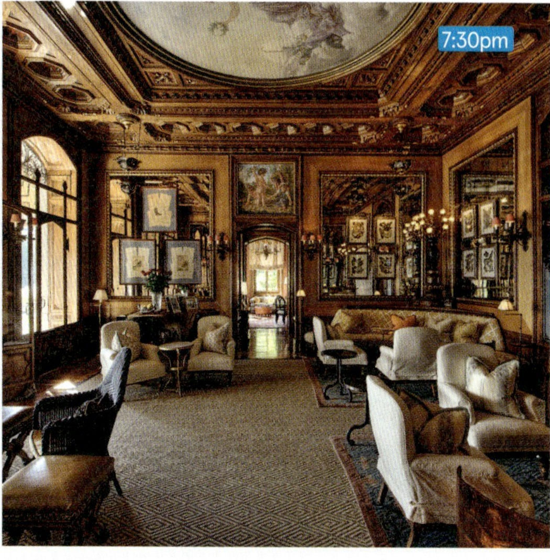

Left: Vittoriale degli Italiani. Above: Villa Feltrinelli.

5:30pm: Music at tea-time

Around 1900 the aristocracy honoured the *lago* with its presence. Testimony to the grandeur of old can be found in ⓫ Gardone Riviera: the Grand Hotel Gardone and the Grand Hotel Fassone. Take a stroll to the Villa Florida, too, and relax over a cup of tea: you can even choose a song or two from Gianmario Cipani's small but exquisite collection of LPs!

6:30pm: The Palace-on-the-Lake

Now it's time to move on to Lake Garda's 'Schönbrunn Palace'. This is the nickname given to the Villa Bettoni in Bogliaco due to its exuberant pomp. Unfortunately it can only be viewed from the outside as it is still the private residence of the Bettoni family.

7pm: Promenading along the lakeside

A short walk through 15 Gargnano, a couple of miles further on, reveals a *grandezza* of a different kind – namely that of the lake itself.

7:30pm: A two-starred finale

Treat yourself to dinner in the only 2 Michelin-starred restaurant on the lake: the Villa Feltrinelli – also considered one of the best hotels in Europe. Only if you have reserved in advance (www.villafeltrinelli.com) will you be allowed in – sheer elegance with perfect service. *Grandezza* indeed!

1 ★★ Sirmione

Why	Jutting out into the lake and yet joined to the mainland – that's something only Sirmione can offer
Don't Miss	Climb the 47m (154ft)-high *mastio* – it's well worth the effort
Time	Plan a whole day to explore this delightful little town
Tip	Very good Lugana white wine comes from a village of the same name nearby

If you leave the A4 *autostrada* at the Sirmione/San Martino exit, you will reach Colombare, a pristine if undistinguished village where a road heads off to Sirmione. This 4km (2mi) drive starts straightforwardly enough, but soon the peninsula narrows dramatically and reaches a car park (Sirmione is off-limits to all but essential vehicles so you have to leave your car here) and there, ahead of you, is one of the most magical places on the lake.

Entry to the town is by drawbridge and through the gate in the 13th-century walls built by the Scaligeri, the Lords of Verona. Although the Romans were here first, the walls and the castle date from the time of the Scaligeri.

The Moated Castle

The Rocca Scaligera was built by Mastino I della Scala as a garrison and harbour for his fleet of galleys. Dante is reputed

The view from the main tower on Rocca Scaligera is simply breathtaking.

to have stayed here and artists by the dozen came to admire it and draw inspiration. The American poet Ezra Pound met the Irish novelist James Joyce here. Although the castle is now empty it is worth a visit for the view from the central tower that rises 27m (89ft) above the lake. The Scaligeri fishtail battlements seen on the walls and towers of the Rocca are a familiar sight around the lake. The museum houses some beautiful galleys excavated from the River Oglio.

Sirmione's Rocca Scaligera was built in the 13th century partly of stone and partly of brick to protect the Old Town on the lake

The Old Town

North of the castle the town of Sirmione is crammed into about half the 70ha (173 acres) of the peninsula and comprises a maze of alleyways and streets with occasional views of the lake, olive trees or cypresses. To the right, as you head away from the castle, is the church of Santa Maria Maggiore from the 15th century. The builders incorporated a Roman capital in the porticoed façade.

Continuing through the town you will reach the Catullo Spa, the thermal water that first brought the Romans to the peninsula. Rising from under the lake at a temperature of 69°C (156°F), the sulphurous water is said to be excellent for the treatment of both muscular and sinus problems. The waters are piped to several hotels in the town that offer thermal treatments to guests.

Near the Catullo Spa is San Pietro in Mavino, begun in the 8th century on the site of a temple but rebuilt in about 1000. The church has some good frescoes by the Verona School from the early medieval period. Note *The Last Judgment* (14th century) in particular.

There are places to swim and sunbathe at the head of the island, at the Lido delle Bionde and near the flat limestone terraces at Punta Grotte that extend just above or below the surface of the water around the cape. Some of the best panoramic views of the lake can be had from here, taking in a view to the east and west around the 'belly' and to the north.

Rocca Scaligera

The mighty moated castle of the della Scala family dating from around 1300 is Sirmione's most distinctive landmark and the most important fortified site on Lake Garda.

❶ Masonry: The walls are made of bricks fired locally and natural stone from Cortine Hill nearby.

❷ Gateway and drawbridge: On the gateway you can see where the drawbridge that was once here was closed using a pulley system. The long rods or gaffs disappeared into slits in the wall, as can be seen above the gateway. The pivotal point was in the slits. At the far end there were chains fixed to the bridge. As the inner ends of the beams were pulled downwards, the bridge lifted upwards.

❸ Inner courtyard: The rectangular inner courtyard is surrounded by thick walls.

❹ Tower complex: The corner towers are connected by a *chemin de ronde* – or protective walkway – accessed by a flight of steps. The 47m (154ft)-high main tower, the *mastio*, provides wonderful views of the southern end of the lake.

5 Harbour: The large crenellated castle harbour is unique, not only on Lake Garda but among all European fortresses in Europe. Once used for supplies and defensive purposes, it is now full of water lilies.

The Grotti di Catullo are the ruins of a Roman villa

Surfing is really the preserve of the north, but the lower end of the lake is inviting due to the temperature of the water and is ideal for fair-weather surfers.

Grotte di Catullo

The name may give you the wrong impression as these are not caves nor was it where the poet Catullus lived. In one of his works he calls Sirmione the 'very eye of all peninsulas and isles that in our lakes of silver lie'. These are the remains of a representative Roman guest house or the large villa of a wealthy man. The name 'grotte' (lit. caves) was coined by a chronicler during the Renaissance to describe the tumble-down, overgrown complex. At that time it was though that this may have been the site of Catullus' residence. The beautiful location on the white cliffs above Lake Garda and the vast extent of the complex over more than 20,000m² (215,000ft²) – the largest of its kind in Italy – are unique indeed.

The villa was built in 150AD and probably fell into ruin in the 4th century. Ignoring the extensions to the north and south, the main villa is rectangular and measures 167.5 × 105m (550 × 344ft). As the site is not flat, a lower level was constructed under sections of the building, sometimes cutting into the rock. It is largely this basement that can be seen today; nothing now remains of the two floors of grand rooms above. Olive trees, rosemary, thyme, mint and oregano now grow among the ruins and emit an intensive smell.

INSIDER TIP The **Bar Ai Cigni** at Vittorio Emanuele 12 is excellent und especially well known for its ice cream.

186 C2

Castello Scaligero (Rocca Scaligera)
☎ 030 91 64 68 April–Sep 9–7, Oct–March Tue–Sun 9–4
€4

Grotte di Catullo and Museo
☎ 030 91 61 57
www.grottedicatullo.beniculturali.it
April–Sep Tue–Sat 8:30–7; Sun 9:30–6:30; Oct–March Tue–Sat until 5, Sun until 2 €6

Salò

Why	Salò has the most beautiful lungolago on the lake
When	In the morning due to the warm, atmospheric morning light on the Bay of Salò
Time	You can see all the sights in a morning unless...
Tip	...you want to spend some time shopping!

The mild climate and beautiful location on a gently sweeping bay protected from the wind at the foot of 569m (1867ft)-high Monte San Bartolomeo, where vines, bay and olive trees grow on its slopes, was appreciated by the Romans too. Today, Salò's one-way system soon becomes a labyrinth – it's best to park outside the Old Town.

Under the Romans who called the settlement they founded *Salodium* and the Visconti from Milan, who turned Salò into their administrative seat in the 14th century, as well as under the Venetians (1405–1797), the town developed into the political centre on the western shore and a pivotal point in the region. Later, the mild climate also attracted the

Strolling along Salò's lakeside promenade

Top: View of Salò and Monte Baldo on the opposite shore.
Above: In the Museo di Salò exhibits include a bust of the violin maker Gasparo da Salò and the Biondo violine contrabasso.
Left: The interior of Salò cathedral.

aristocracy and the rich from northern Europe. In 1901 an earthquake struck the area. In the years to follow, the old town centre was completely rebuilt and a new lakeside promenade created on wooden piles driven into the bed of the lake.

The Republic of Salò

The town hit the headlines in World War I when it became the seat of the Repubblica Sociale Italiana from 1943 until 1945, the last fascist government in Italy, set up with help from the Germans. It started with the arrest of Benito Mussolini in 1943. In a risky undertaking, Hitler ordered Mussolini to be freed from his prison in the Abruzzi and made head of a puppet regime based in Salò and Gargnano.

The Ministry of Culture was established in Salò and the Foreign Ministry moved into what is now the Hotel Laurin. In April 1945, Salò was bombarded by the Allies from the eastern shore and, on 29 April, Mussolini fled to Lake Como where he and his mistress Clara Petacci were later executed by partisans.

Duomo

Among the maze of squares and narrow streets of the Old Town is the *duomo*, Santa Maria Annunziata, one of the finest late-Gothic buildings on the lake. Inside, the dark stone contrasts with several strongly lit paintings, including works by Romanino and Zenon Veronese, and a golden polyptych by Paolo Veneziano. In summer, concerts are given on the square in front of the cathedral.

Museums

Objects excavated from the Roman *Salodium* are exhibited in Salò's Museo Civico Archeologico while the Museo di Salò focuses on the town's history and past residents and includes instruments made by the violin maker Gasparo da Salò (1540–1609) and several anatomical specimens once owned by the surgeon Giovan Battista Rinio (1795–1856) who was also born in Salò.

The complex also includes the Museo del Nastro Azzurro – a military museum – at Via Fantoni 49, with exhibits from the Napoleonic times up until 1945. One room is devoted to the Salò Republic. *Nastro Azzuro* means 'blue ribbon'. Although the colours of the Italian flag are red, green and white, Italy's national colour is blue.

INSIDER TIP The most delicious organic ice cream on the lake can be found at **Casa del Dolce** on the cathedral square.

---

186 B3

Museo Civico Archeologico
Via Fantoni 49
0365 21423
Mon–Fri 10–noon
€2

Museo di Salò (MuSa), Museo del Nastro Azzurro
Via Brunati 9 0365 20553
www.museodisalo.it
March–May, Oct, Nov Tue–Sun 10–7, June–Sep Tue–Sun 10–8
€14

⓫ Gardone Riviera

Why	Nowhere else on the lake is the nostalgic feeling for the *grandezza* of old so omnipresent
When	To avoid the worst of the queues at Il Vittoriale arrive at 9am
Time	One day (including Vittoriale)
Tip	Mussolini had a (love) nest in the Torre San Marco

Tranquil Gardone Riviera was already considered one of the most elegant addresses on Lake Garda in the 19th century. Elegant hotels, lavish summer residences and magnificent villas with beautiful park-like grounds still characterise the little town today.

The commune of Gardone comprises four settlements: Gardone Sotto, Gardone Sopra, Fasano Sotto and Fasano Sopra.

As the slopes of Monte Lavino (907m/2975ft), Pizzocolo (1583m/5194ft) and Monte Spino (1468m/4816ft) come right down virtually to the edge of the lake, the elegant hotels in Gardone Riviera are squeezed along the shore. The old village centre, Gardone Sopra, nestles on a green slope above the Gardesana (Corso Zanardelli). The mountains protect it from the cool Tramontana winds, giving it a Mediterranean climate that made it possible to lay out a beautiful botanic garden. To the south, Gardone and Salò almost merge with each other, with *palazzi* hidden behind the palm trees, cypresses and oleanders that link the two settlements.

Lungolago D'Annunzio

The wide but relatively short promenade is lined with restaurants and cafés. Between the two Grand Hotels, the Gardone (1884) and the Fasano (1888) is San Marco Tower where Mussolini secretly met his lover, Clara Petacci.

From Giardino Botanico to Vittoriale

Visitors to the Heller Garden (Giardino Botanico) can explore a wonderful labyrinth of narrow, twisting paths leading through the thick vegetation, passing artificially created streams and lily ponds, crossed by little wooden

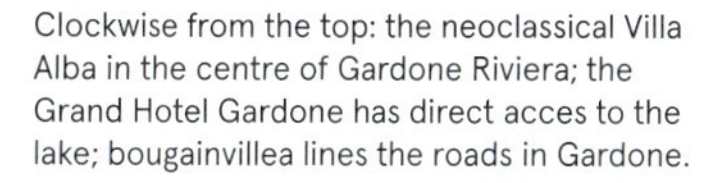

Clockwise from the top: the neoclassical Villa Alba in the centre of Gardone Riviera; the Grand Hotel Gardone has direct acces to the lake; bougainvillea lines the roads in Gardone.

bridges. Benches in hidden corners invite visitors to relax for a few minutes among papyrus, lotus flowers and bamboo.

The park was laid out in 1900 around his villa by the dentist and botanist Arthur Hruska (1880–1971) from Austria. He planted some 2000 plants from all climatic zones on earth. The centrepiece of the garden is a miniature landscape made of stone from the Dolomites. The Austrian artist André Heller bought the estate in the 1980s as it was starting to get overgrown. The sculptures in the garden are from him and artist friends like Mimmo Palladino. The park is divided thematically and starts with the Asian section, followed by zones focussing on Alpine, scented and medicinal plants.

The Giardino Botanico is now owned by the André Heller Foundation.

From the car park a flight of steps next to the Giardino Botanico leads up to Gardone Sopra and to Il Vittoriale. Just before the entrance to Il Vittoriale is the church of San Nicolà (1740) with wonderful views over the lake to be had from the terrace outside. The inside boasts several frescos and a lot of decorative plasterwork.

Vittoriale degli Italiani

"An almost frantic intoxication of colour and atmosphere" (Hugo von Hoffmannsthal) prevails in Gabriele d'Annunzio's poems.

Gabriele d'Annunzio (1863–1938) was a prominent, powerfully eloquent Italian poet, a 'war hero' and successful Casanova who called himself an 'interpreter of human madness'. From 1921 until his death, D'Annunzio lived with his wife and several lovers in his whimsical villa on Lake Garda. Politically he felt close to Mussolini when he was still an unknown Socialist. D'Annunzio's proximity to fascism, his excessive, unconventional lifestyle and his egocentricity cast a shadow over his work as a writer. He published his first volume of poems at the age of 16 and became well-known after the publication of *Il Piacere* (The Child of Pleasure) in 1889 – a novel influenced by Nietzsche. His strength lay in his receptiveness for literary movements and especially for French Symbolism. He confessed his attraction to a heathen cult of the senses and of beauty and, as such, became one of Italy's most controversial lyricists.

'Vittoriale degli Italiani' (The Shrine of Italian Victories) is what d'Annunzio called the estate that he created more as a whimsical place of self-adulation than anything else. The complex includes a large park (Il Vittoriale) and the poet's residence (Casa d'Annunzio). Visitors first past the open-air theatre where concerts are held and ballets and plays performed in July and August. In the 'Schifamondo Wing' (meaning 'disdain of the world') there is a small museum with photographs, writings and mementoes of the poet and an auditorium. The SVA plane from which d'Annunzio dropped propaganda leaflets over Vienna during World War I is suspended from the ceiling.

A path between the main house and the Schifamondo leads to the park which is scattered with items recalling d'Annunzio's military achievements and experiences such

D'Annunzio's house, the so-called Priora (priory), is stuffed full of artworks, kitsch and curiosities and can only be visited on a guided tour (top and above left). Right: The 'stranded' bow of a navy battleship lies in the poet's garden

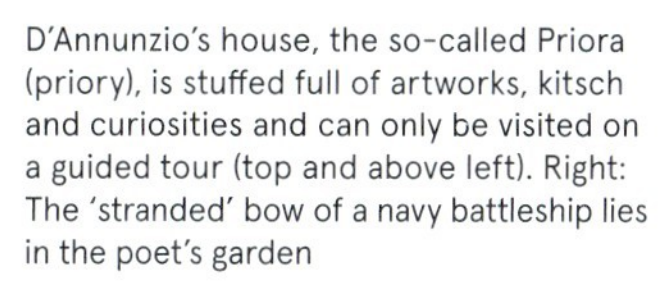

as the MAS speedboat and the massive bow of the battleship 'Puglia'. Further up is the gleaming white mausoleum containing the mable sarcophagus with the vain inscription: 'War Hero'.

INSIDER TIP If you order a cup of tea or coffee in the **Villa Florida**, a song will be played for you on the old record player on the bar free of charge (Corso Giuseppe Zanardelli 113, hotelvillaflorida.co.uk).

A180 B3

Heller Garden
☎ 336 41 08 77
www.hellergarden.com
Mid-March–mid-Oct 9–7 €9

Il Vittoriale degli Italiani
☎ 0365 29 65 11
www.vittoriale.it
April–Sep 9–7, Nov–March 9–4
from €8, depending on the length of the visit

At Your Leisure

12 Lago di Ledro

Lake Ledro can be reached by taking the well signposted tunnel that by-passes the centre of Riva. Bronze Age dwellings were found on the lake where a replica dwelling can be seen in Molina di Ledro, the village at the eastern end of the lake. A museum here (Museo delle Palafitte) includes displays on how people lived at that time. Beyond Molina the main road closely follows the north shore of the lake where you can turn off and visit the Lago d'Idro and Lago di Valvestino. You can return to Riva via Gargnano along the west shore of the lake – a lovely day trip.

186 C/D3
Museo delle Palafitte
0464 50 81 82
www.palafitteled ro.it
March–June and Sep–Nov 9–5; July–Aug 10–6 €3.50

13 Limone sul Garda

Limone once boasted the most extensive lemon groves in the whole region. The reputation of this tourist honeypot on Lake Garda is however not due to the fruit but its beautiful Old Town and unique location. Its name in fact almost certainly derives from the Roman word *limes*, meaning a border – Limone having once been a border town between Italy and Austria.

The old harbour in Limone sul Garda

The church of Madonna di Monte Castello, near Tignale

Lemons and also citrons – a lemon-like fruit used in the production of *acqua di cedro*, a lemon brandy – and other citrus fruits were grown on terraces above the lake; the trees being enclosed in greenhouses (*limonaie*) during the winter to protect them from frost. With the unification of Italy, Sicily soon replaced Limone as the chief producer of lemons.

The coming of the Gardesana Occidentale ensured Sirmione's development as a tourist resort – up until 1931 it could only be reached by boat. The wide lakeside promenade, Lungolago Marconi, lined by numerous souvenir shops, cafés and bars, leads to the Piazza Garibaldi at the centre. Just a few yards further on, the old harbour – a small basin surrounded by buildings smothered with flowers – comes as a surprise.

Limone hit the headlines in 1979 when Professor Cesare Sirtori of Milan discovered an unusual protein, called the Apolipoprotein A1 Milano, a gene that rids the arteries of fats and so virtually eliminates arteriosclerosis and heart disease. As a result, Limone has the highest concentration of over-80s in the whole of Italy.

187 D4

14 Tremosine & Tignale

High above the lake, between Limone and Gargnano further to the south, are Tremosine and Tignale plateaus where flower-filled meadows, wooded slopes, rock faces, high hills and small villages combine to make one of the most beautiful areas on Lake Garda. This is a region to be explored on a leisurely drive or even on foot. If you have lunch or a cup of coffee on the nerve-racking 'Terrazza del Brivido' in Pieve be prepared for the 400m (1312ft) sheer drop into the depths below. But if you only have a short time choose a day when the air is clear and take the road to Tignale off the Gardesana Occidentale to the north of Gargnano. There are a number of view points along this road from which the lake and Monte

Baldo can be admired. A few miles further on, a short, steep road leads to the church of Madonna di Montecastello, built on the ruins of a Scaligeri castle and famed for its view and works of art. These include four paintings on copper attributed to Palma the Younger and a fresco of the Madonna and Child that some authorities claim is by Giotto.

↝ 186 C4 (Tignale)
↝ 186 C4 (Tremosine)
Madonna di Monte Castello
☎ 036 57 30 20 ◑ Easter–Oct daily 9:30–6 🎟 Free

15 Gargnano

To the north of the centre, on the Gardesana, is the parish church of San Martino that was built in 1837 in the Italian Classicist style. Narrow lanes lead down to the lake and the pretty little harbour. During the Risorgimento (1866), French and Italian ships retreated to this spot and were bombarded from the lake by six Austrian gunboats. The scars caused at that time can still be seen on the 16th-century Palazzo Comunale (the old town hall) near the harbour.

Paradise has a name: Gargnano

Benito Mussolini ruled the 'Republic of Salò' from his office in the Palazzo Feltrinelli at the northern end of the lakeside promenade. The Neo-Renaissance palace is now owned by the University of Milan. Just a little further on is La Fontanella park with a pebbly beach and concrete platforms for sunbathing and swimming.

Beyond is the former summer residence, the Villa Feltrinelli, of the Feltrinelli family which made a fortune in timber and publishing. It is now a luxury hotel. The church of San Francesco, with its single nave, lies to the south of the harbour in the Via Roma. The Franciscan order established a house of prayer and monastery here from 1289 onwards, of which only the façade of the church and the cloisters have survived, while the church was given its present appearance in the 17th century. The Romanesque and Late Gothic cloister is delightful.

↝ 186 C3
Church of San Francesco & Cloister
☎ 036 57 10 17 ◑ 8–8 🎟 Free

Magical Moment

Out on the Lake with the Fishermen

You have to have booked in advance, but if you are among the lucky few, you will experience something you will never forget. At around 3.45am the Dominici family of fishers from San Giacomo near Gargnano set off across the lake that is still pitch black at this time of the morning. Marco, his brother Luca and their father Umberto only speak Italian and do not take more than two extra people on board.

Information in the office of the mayor of Gargnano, tel: 0365 79 12 43, info@comune.gargnano.bs.it, or direct: Umberto Dominici & figli, tel: 0365 72 0 49.

Lake Garda's own 'Schönbrunn Palace': the Palazzo Bettoni in Bogliaco.

16 Villa & Bogliaco

There are twelve other little settlements that go to make up Gargnano, including Villa and Bogliaco that link up to the south along the shore. The other hamlets cling to the slope above the main village. One house on the main lane in Villa was where the English writer D. H. Lawrence (1885–1930) lived and worked for a year. From San Tommaso's church above, there is a lovely view of the lake.

The most prominent building in Bogliaco is the Palazzo Bettoni (not open to the public). The magnificent, three-winged palace with an impressive façade overlooking the lake, has been cut off from its park by the through road. Modelled on the Palace of Schönbrunn in Vienna, it was built around 1750 for Conte Giovanni Bettoni, a general in the cavalry in the service of Maria Theresia. Bogliaco has a beautiful golf course, founded in 1912 (www.golfbogliaco.com). A little further south is the modern Marina di Bogliaco. This is where the Centomiglia starts – the largest sailing regatto on the lake with around 250 competitors held every year.

186 C3

17 Lago di Valvestino

From Gargnano a road winds up through a series of hairpin bends to Val Toscolano and Lago di Valvestino, a man-made reservoir, that often lies shrouded in clouds in the mountain valley. From the lake's far end the valley leads northwards. There are no places to go for a swim but, climbing steeply to the village of Magasa, you will reach the perfect place from which to start beautiful hikes through this dramatic, scenic landscape.

186 C4

18 Lago d'Idro

Continuing westwards from Lago di Valvestino, or heading through the lovely Val Sabbia from Salò, you will reach the town of Idro which shares its name with the lake on which it stands. Have a look at the church of San Michele, with its finely carved high altar, the organ case and the choristers' seats in the choir. From Idro, a road follows the eastern edge of the lake to the village of Vesta where it ends. The views from here to the foothills of the Alps are superb.

On the western side of the lake the road burrows its way through the hills to Anfo. The privately owned castle was Giuseppe Garibaldi's headquarters during his campaign to add Veneto to the kingdom of Italy. The church of San Antonio has a 12th-century *campanile* and excellent Renaissance frescoes.

180 B4

19 Toscolano-Maderno

The little town of Toscolano-Maderno is made up of two settlements divided by the mouth of the River Toscolano – Maderno to the south and Toscolano to the north. With its crescent-shaped bay, long lakeside promenade and attractive villas, as well as an old town centre and harbour, Maderno definitely has more to offer than Toscolano that is really only appealing to campers. Maderno is the western terminus for Garda's car ferry (to Torri del Benaco).

Attractions in the twin-town include the former paper mills, the paper museum and the Orto Botanico Ghirardi with glasshouses full of tropical plants. On the Piazza San Marco near the harbour is the noteworthy Romanesque church of Sant'Andrea Apostolo, built in 1140, with a Late Gothic *campanile* (1469). To the left of the church is the Via Benamati that leads through the Old Town to the River Toscolano, passing the ruins of a Roman villa (no. 79) with a flight of steps set in an enchanting garden. The parish church of Sant'Ercolano is just a few yards further on. It was built on the site of a fortess in the mid 18th century and its tower was converted into a bell tower.

186 C3

Paper Museum
Via Valle delle Cartiere www.valledellecartiere.it April–Sep 10–6, Oct Sat, Sun 10–5 €7
Orto Botanico Ghirardi
Via Religione 0365 64 12 46 May–Sep Wed, Fri 4:30–6:30, Sat 10:30–12:30 Free

20 Isola del Garda

Just off the San Fermo promontory, the 1km (0.6mi)-long Isola del Garda – the largest island on Lake Garda – rises out of the water. It is privately owned by the Borghese-Cavazza family who live in a beautiful villa set in the middle of a landscaped

A jewel on Lake Garda – the villa of the Counts of Borghese-Cavazza on Isola del Garda

park. The island can be visited on a 2-hour guided tour.

> 186 C3 Ferries run April–Oct to the island from ten different harbours. For departure times, see www.isoladelgarda.com €27–32, for the crossing, guided tour and refreshments

21 Desenzano del Garda

The old harbour basin in this, the largest town on Lake Garda, is separated from the port area by a low bridge. The Venetian Palazzo Todeschini facing the harbour was once a grain store. It now houses the tourist information office. Adjoining the lakeside promenade, Lungolago Cesare Battisti, a sarcophagus can be seen that served as a tomb for the Roman Atilia Urbica. The cafés and restaurants right behind the harbour on the Piazza Malvezzi are an inviting place to sit in the shade of the low arcades. The monument in the middle of the square is dedicated to the patron saint of the town, Santa Angela Merici, who founded the Order of St Ursula in 1535. The Duomo Santa Maria Maddalena, built by the architect Giulio Todeschini (1524–1603) in the Late Renaissance style, is on the north side of the *piazza*. The ruins of three Roman buildings were unearthed in the middle of a residential area (Via Crocefisso 22). The excavated site is especially famous for its mosaic floors, now housed in a museum.

> 186 B2
> **Villa Romana**
> Via Crocefisso 22 030 9 14 35 47
> Easter–Sep Tue–Sun 8:30–7:30; Oct–Easter Tue–Sat 8:30–7:30, Sun 8:30–4 €4
> **Museo Archeologico Rambotti**
> Santa Maria de Senioribus, Via Anelli
> 030 9 14 45 29 www.museiarcheologici.net Tue 9–13, Thu, Fri 3–7, Sat, Sun 2:30–7 €4

The beach in Desenzano: this is where rowers uphold an ancient tradition that was brought here from La Serenissima

Where to... Stay

Expect to pay per double room, per night
€ under €80
€€ €80–€150
€€€ over €150

GARDONE RIVIERA

Grand Hotel Fasano €€€
The 3-acre park-like grounds, with banana plants, magnolias and cypresses, run down to the lakeside and include a swimming pool and sunbeds under palm trees. All 75 modern rooms have parquet floors; very good spa facilities, 4 restaurants, car park with surveillance and an array of things to hire, e. g. motorboat, Alfa vintage car, mountain bikes, etc.
186 B3 Via Zanardelli 190
0365 29 02 20 www.ghf.it
Closed mid-Oct to March

Villa Florida €€€
The pink-washed villa and the 27m (90ft) pool perch on terraces, each with a breath-taking view of the lake and the Isola del Garda. Suites or apartments only; all 25 have their own balconies and a view of the lake. Breakfast is not merely served but celebrated on the panoramic terrace Belvedere dell'Angelo.
186 B3 Via Zanardelli 113
0365 2 18 36 www.hotelvillaflorida.com
Closed mid-Oct to March

GARGNANO

Lefay Resort & Spa €€€

The most beautiful resort in the *Limonaia* style high above Gargnano and the lake with magnificent views. Suites only; 2 restaurants (also for low-calorie diets) Two outdoor pools, an excellent spa, with one suite on the lake with its own private pool.
186 C3 Via Feltrinelli 136
0365 24 18 00 www.lefayresorts.com

LIMONE SUL GARDA

S Lido €€
Friendly and comfortable, right on the lake. Half board only.
187 D4 Via IV Novembre 36
03 65 95 45 74 www.lidohotel.com
Closed Oct to April 15

SALÒ

Duomo €€
Fantastic location, 24 lovely rooms with views of the cathedral or the lake, restaurant.
186 B3 Lungolago Zanardelli 63
0365 2 10 26 www.hotelduomosalo.it

SIRMIONE

Flaminia €€€
In the Old Town right on the lake. Lovely sun terrace.
186 C2 Piazza Flaminia 8
030 91 60 78
www.hotelflaminia.it

Villa Cortine €€€
Small *grand hôtel* in a beautiful villa with peaceful gardens.
186 C2 Via Grotte 6
030 9 90 58 90
www.palacehotelvillacortine.com
Closed Oct to March

TREMOSINE

S Village Hotel Lucia €
A hotel and holiday 'village' with a pool and lovely view of the lake on the edge of Tremosine.
186 C4 Via del Sole 2
0365 95 30 88 www.hotellucia.it
Closed Oct to March

Where to... Eat and Drink

Expect to pay for a three-course meal for one, excluding drinks and service
€ under €30
€€ €30–€50
€€€ over €50

DESENZANO DEL GARDA

Ristorante Pizzeria Kapperi €
A modern and spacious pizzeria. Freshly made pasta dishes are a speciality.
186 B2 Via N. Sauro 7 030 9 99 18 93
www.kapperi.eu Closed Mon

GARDONE RIVIERA

Il Fagiano €€€
Matteo Felter, the chef, was born on Lake Garda and uses the products his native lake has to offer: fish, vegetables, olive oil. And he creates miniature works of art that are of Michelin star quality. The €85 tasting menu is well worth trying!
186 B2 Via Zanardelli 190 (at Grand Hotel Fasano) 0365 29 02 20 www.ghf.it
Dinner only (booking is essential), closed Nov–March

Trattoria da Marietta €€
A short walk from Il Vittoriale, this is an unpretentious and friendly place. Excellent food and a good wine list. Delicious pizzas are also served.
186 B3 Via Montecucco 78
037 77 08 16 22 www.trattoriamarietta.it
Closed Mon

Villa Fiordaliso €€€
A meal here is one of the great dining experiences on the western shore: wickedly expensive, wickedly good. The restaurant with rooms is in an elegant villa. The cooking, service and wine list are first-class. Booking is essential.
186 B3 Corso Zanardelli 150
036 52 01 58 www.villafiordaliso.it
Closed Mon and Tue lunch, and mid-Nov to March

GARGNANO

La Tortuga €€€
Michelin-star restaurant.
186 C3 Via XXIV. Maggio 5 0365 7 12 51
www.ristorantelatortuga.it
Closed Tue, and Nov to Feb

PIEVE DI TREMOSINE

Miralago €€
Possibly the best-positioned restaurant on the top of the cliff in Pieve di Tremosine. On a clear day the view is sensational. Straightforward cooking excellently presented. Some dishes include local chestnuts and mushrooms, each of which should be tried.
186 C4 Piazza Cozzaglio 2
0365 95 30 01 www.miralago.it
Closed Tue and mid-Dec to mid-Jan

SALÒ

La Campagnola €€€
Delicious fish from Lake Garda: trout, tench, pike, whitefish.
186 B3 Via Brunati 11 036 52 21 53
www.lacampagnola1952.it Closed Mon

Osteria di Mezzo €€
On a road that runs parallel to the promenade, this little restaurant has a simple menu (homemade pizzas) with well-prepared food and friendly service.
186 B3 Via di Mezzo 10 036 5 29 09 66
www.osteriadimezzo.it Closed Tue

SIRMIONE

Vecchia Lugana €€€
A place for gourmets who want to spoil themselves right on the lake. Typical Lake Garda fare, superbly cooked and presented. In the wine-growing village of Lugana.
186 B3 Piazzale Vecchia Lugana 1
030 91 90 12 Closed Mon, Tue

Trattoria La Fiasca €
Charming restaurant in the fortress. Simple but good.
186 C2 Via Santa Maria Maggiore 11
030 9 90 61 11 www.trattorialafiasca.it

Where to... Shop

Most of the towns and villages on Lake Garda's western shore are small, with limited shopping potential, with the exception of Salò and Desenzano. Cafés, restaurants, souvenir shops and a few conventional outlets dominate the centre of many villages.

There are good weekly markets at Desenzano del Garda (Tue), Limone (Tue, April–Oct), Manerba (Fri), Salò (Sat), Sirmione (Fri), Toscolano Maderno (Thu). There is also an excellent antiques market in Desenzano del Garda on the first Sunday of the month (except Aug).

DESENZANO DEL GARDA

Cashmere Ironia (Via Porto Vecchio) sells tempting sweaters and scarves from its own production line whereas Intimamente (Piazza Matteotti Giacomo 5) has designer underclothes for men and women.

For jewellery go to Gioielleria Franzoni (Via Roma 16). For leather try Martinetti (Via Generale Achille Papa 40), particularly for handbags and belts, and La Bagagerie, (Via Porto Vecchio 22).

If you are interested in art, try Galleria Zacchi La Cornice (Piazza Giuseppe Malvezzi 45) which has interesting modern artworks in wood, metal and ceramics, as well as paintings on wood.

Shopping in Salò

GARDONE RIVIERA

Enoteca Bedussi (Corso Repubblica 40) sells a large collection of wines, spirits and local liqueurs.

Antique Marino (Piazza Marconi 6) has a good range of antiques.

LIMONE

There are a small number of souvenir shops and cheap outlets in the town, the best of which is Raffi (Lungolago Marconi 48) which sells more stylish designer clothes.

SALÒ

For handbags and elegant jewellery try Tranquilli (Via San Carlo 58), elegant fashions can be found at MR (Via S. Carlo 39), and for shoes try Principe (Lungolago Zanardelli 21).

GB Argento (Via Fantoni 10) has a superb range of silverware, Quartiere Chic (Via Fantoni 1) kitchenware and linens for the home and Ottica Scotti (Piazza G Zanardelli 7) gold, silver and crystal.

You'll find the best antiques at Negoziuo d'Arte da Marinella (Lungolago Zanardelli 29/30)

Colorificio Nastuzzo (Via Fantoni 35) sells artists' materials and offers watercolour courses.

SIRMIONE

Clothes and fashion boutiques can be found on the Via Vittorio Emanuele, linking the castle and the Catullo Thermal and a few of the side streets.

Other outlets include Art Gallery Donavil (Via Dante 15) for Chinese antiques, English silverware and Murano glass.

L'Enoteca (Corte Salvelli 6) and Enoteca Il Volto (Via Piana 16) both have a huge range of wines.

Head for Sogni Profumati (Piazza Castello 12) where there is an amazing collection of soaps, candles and perfumes, and Più Gioielli, (Via Vittorio Emanuele 54) for jewellery, particularly amber.

Where to... Go Out

SPORT AND LEISURE

Watersports

Sailing and windsurfing schools can be found in Sirmione – among the best are Martini, tel: 030 91 62 08 and Centro Surf Sirmione, tel: 030 9 19 61 30–, Desenzano (Fraglia Vela, tel: 030 9 14 33 43) and Campione (Vela Club, tel: 0365 91 69 08).
The Centomiglia Sailing Competition (www.centomiglia.it), held at Gargnano in September, is one of Europe's premier events and attracts entries from far and wide.
Diving is good at the southern end of the lake and there are several schools in Desenzano, including Tritone Sub (tel: 338 4 46 55 70). Boat hire is available in most of the lake towns.

Adventure Sports

Hiking on Tremosine-Tignale is wonderful, and the plateaus also offer more adventurous opportunities with parasailing and canyoning.

Golf

There are few courses on the western shore. The Club Palazzo Arzaga (www.arzaga-golf-garda.com) near Padenghe (just north of Desenzano) has 18-hole and 9-hole courses.
Close by, at Soiano del Lago there are 18-hole and 9-hole courses at the Garda Golf Country Club (www.gardagolf.it). There is also a 18-hole course at Bogliaco Golf Resort (www.golfbogliaco.com) in Toscolano-Maderno.

Mountainbiking

You are almost certain to get wobbly knees if you take the mountain bike stretch from the harbour in Campione di Tremosine to Pieve di Termosine up on the plateau. The landscape and route itself are stunning. The tour is 23km (14.3mi) long with an altitude difference of 750m (2460ft) overall, with lots of ups and downs. It takes between 4 and 5 hours (www.skyclimber.it).

Spas

Relax in the Terme di Sirmione at Via Punta Staffalo 1 (www.termedisirmione.com).

FESTIVALS

The Estate Musicale del Garda Gasparo da Salò is a classical music festival (July–Sep) with open-air concerts on the Piazza Duomo. Other concerts from July to September are held in Gardone Riviera, Desenzano del Garda and Gargnano. Classical music concerts are also held in Salò's Palazzo Fantoni in May and June and an International Classical Music Festival takes place in August in Manerba. A Guitar Festival is held each September in Gargnano and a Jazz Festival from June to September at Gardone Riviera.

NIGHTLIFE

During the summer there is an open-air cinema and theatre in Desenzano in the Castello. Gargnano also offers an unusual cinema experience: with showings held in the church of San Martino! The best area for discos and music bars is also in and around Desenzano. Of the discos currently open, the best are Art Club (www.artclubdisco.com) at Via Mella 4 and Golden Beach on Spiaggia d'Oro in Via Zamboni (www.goldenbeachdesenzano.com), as well as Fura (www.fura.it) in Via Lavagnone 13.
In Lonato head for Dehor in Via Fornace dei Gorghi 2 (www.dehor.ne).

Summer, sun and fun in the shadow of the castle:
Malcesine is often referred to as the 'pearl of Lake Garda'.

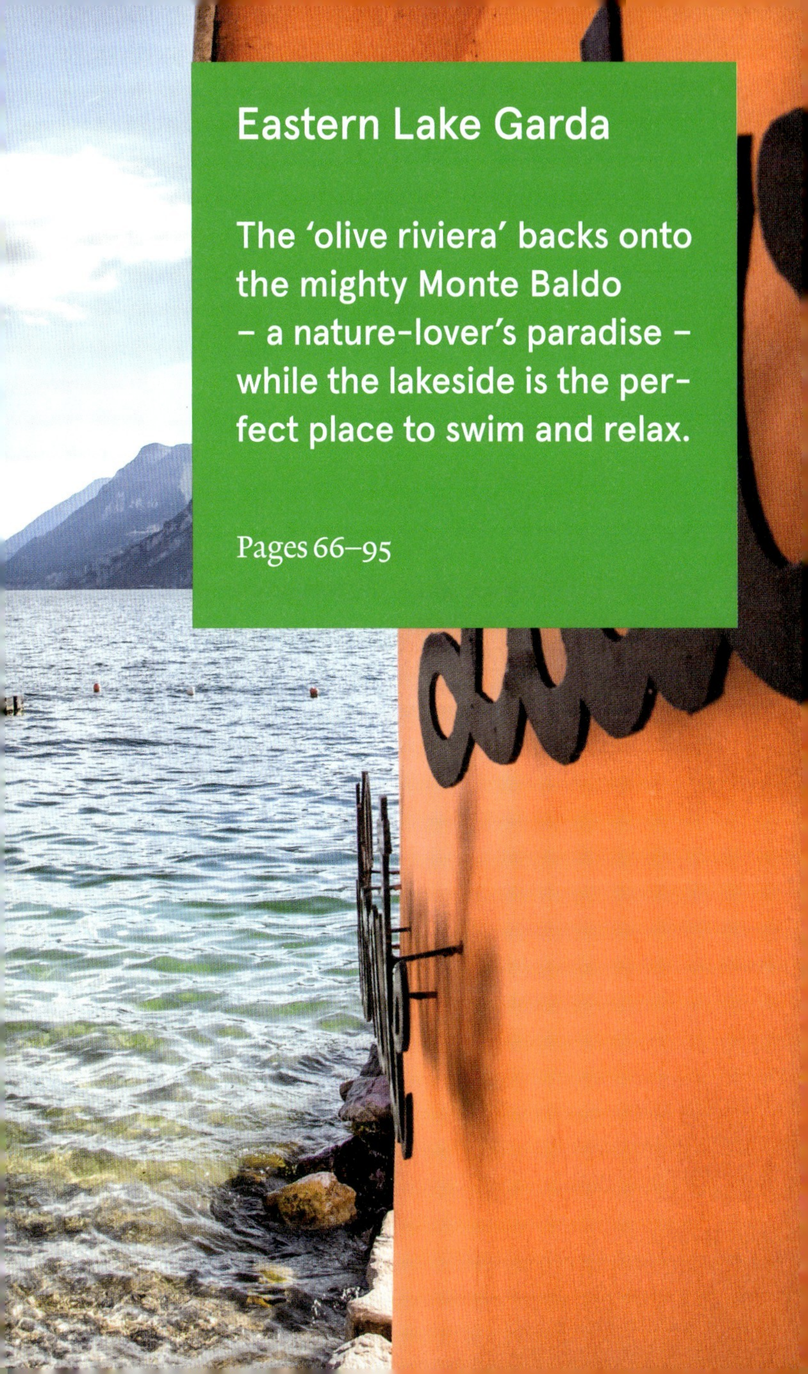

Eastern Lake Garda

The ‘olive riviera’ backs onto the mighty Monte Baldo – a nature-lover’s paradise – while the lakeside is the perfect place to swim and relax.

Pages 66–95

Getting Your Bearings

At first glance it might be said that the western shore of Lake Garda is more for lovers of history and culture, whereas the eastern shore appeals more to sun-lovers and the active visitor. There is an element of truth in that, but both sides of the lake have much more – often unexpected things – to offer.

At the southeastern tip of Lake Garda there are classic entertainment sites such as Gardaland and nearby waterparks. But this is also a land of vines, the famous wines of Bardolino being pressed from grapes grown within sight of the lake. Further inland are the vineyards that produce Valpolicella, one of the great wines of Italy. There is history here too. At Peschiera the Austrians built huge fortifications to maintain their grip on this part of the country.

The strategic importance of the lake is also reflected in the castles that pre-date Austrian Peschiera – Scaligeri castles with their familiar fishtail battlements. Lazise is a fine example, but the best is at Malcesine, its tower having become a symbol of the lake. Between the two is Garda, the town which gave its name to the lake, while beyond Malcesine, at the head of the lake, is Riva del Garda, now an important tourist centre but with a castle that hints at a less peaceful past. History certainly has a place on the eastern shore and, if the east does not match the profusion of villas on the west, it has its natural delights – Monte Baldo, above Malcesine, is one of the best and most accessible mountain ridges on the lake. And the many little wonders to the left and right of the routes you pass should not be overseen: namely the region's famous flora. As Monte Baldo was not covered by a glacier in the Ice Age, many 'relict plants' survived the long period of cold, including a number which are unique to the area.

TOP 10

❷ ★★ Malcesine & Monte Baldo

❸ ★★ Garda

❺ ★★ Riva del Garda

At Your Leisure

22 San Martino della Battaglia & Solferino

23 Parco Giardino Sigurtà

24 Peschiera del Garda

25 Gardaland

26 Lazise

27 Bardolino

28 Punta di San Vigilio

29 Torri del Benaco

30 Nago-Torbole

31 Arco

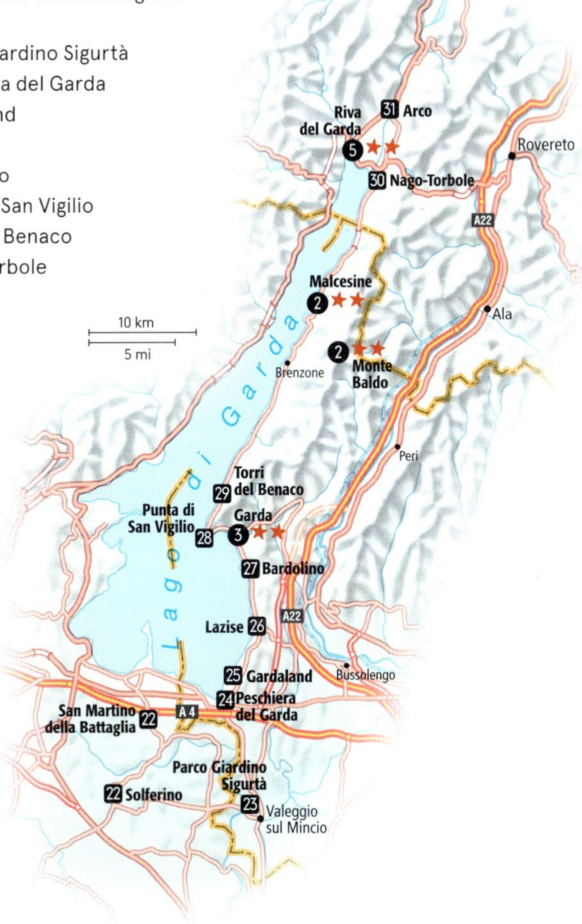

My Day on a bright-red Vespa

Scooters are available to hire in every larger town on Lake Garda, such as in Torbole – the starting point of the next 44km (28mi) along the eastern side of the lake as far as Garda. The good thing is that Vespas up to 125cc can be hired by anyone who has a standard driving licence. So off we go!

10am: For the Love of the Road and la Dolce Vita

Right on the dot when Torbole Vespa Rent (Via Matteotti 54, Nago-Torbole, tel: 0464 505447, www.torbolevesparent.it/it/rent, hire price per day: 57 euros) opens its doors, we take possession of our Vespas for the day. I pick the red one! Paperwork, briefing (the scooters are very simple to ride: accelerate, brake, steer!) and off we go past the pretty customs house in 30 Nago-Torbole heading for the Gardesana direttisimo going south: an unadulterated feeling for the freedom of the road and *la dolce vita* on the SS 249, lined with olive trees and cypresses.

10:30am: Welcome to Arcadia!

In next to nothing we're in Malcesine! What a fantastic ride! Right on the water, with the lake to the right and Monte Baldo to the left. We were pretty tempted just to carry on but the Castello Scaligero in 2 ★★ Malcesine is an absolute must. It was here that Goethe was almost arrested on suspicion of being a spy. The *comune* itself with its twisty, narrow alleyways is well-worth a visit. The many boutiques,

10am: For the Love of the Road and la Dolce Vita
Riva del Garda
Start/ End
30
Vespa Rent
10am/ 7:30pm
Tempesta
10:30am: Welcome to Arcadia!
Campagnola
Castello di Malcesine
10:30am
2
Monte Baldo
Val di Sogno
Cassone
12:15pm
12:15pm: In the Valley of Dreams
:45pm: Stop for a picture in 'orri del Banaco
Isola del Trimelone
Brenzone
12:45pm
12:45pm: A Quick Dip in the Lake
Castelletto di Brenzone
5:30pm: Back up North
5 km
3 mi
5:30pm
4:15pm: Off to the Balcone del Garda
1:45pm
Castello Scaligero
29
San Zeno di Montagna
Balcone del Garda
4:15pm
28
3
3:30pm
3:30 pm: 'The Most Beautiful Spot in the World'

Top: View of Nago-Torbole, the starting point of our tour.
Right: A short stop between Brenzone and Torri del Benaco.

cafés and restaurants are full of people; but without the tourists you get the feeling that this place has changed little over the centuries.

12:15am: In the Valley of Dreams

We zoom past the Isola dell'Olivo on our right before reaching the 'Valley of Dreams', the Val di Sogno, with Isola di Sogno and lots of colourful sailing boats. A real world champion actually founded the first windsurfing school on the lake – and to this day surfing and sailing courses are still held. In Cassone we take a break to look at a river – well, it's more a stream really. What makes the Aril so special is that it's officially Italy's shortest river. Right at its source it has a width of several yards before flowing under several houses and three bridges, forming a miniature lake and a waterfall en route: and all over a distance of just 175m (575ft).

12:45am: A Quick Dip in the Lake

Our route takes us past a mass of different beaches. In Brenzone, with the Isola Trimelone lying peacefully in the lake in front of us, we get of our Vespas and enjoy a quick splash in the water.

1:45pm: Stop for a picture in Torri del Banaco

Another *castello* invites us to get off our scooters, this time in 29 Torri del Benaco. In the car park we take a wonderful selfie with our scooter and the Castello Scaligero that dates

En route we have enough time for a quick dip in the lake (and a bit of sunbathing).

from 1383. For lunch we pick one of the restaurant pontoons on the lake.

3:30pm: 'The Most Beautiful Spot in the World'

In the 16th century, the humanist Agostino di Brenzone described the 28 Punta di San Vigilio as 'the most beautiful spot in the world'. And on such as lovely day as the one we have chosen, it's very easy to agree.

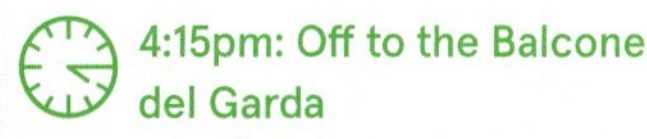

4:15pm: Off to the Balcone del Garda

We reach 3 ★★ Garda. A quick wander along the particularly beautiful *lungolago* eating an ice cream, we set our minds on our return journey. We want to see the 'balcone del Garda' en route and head off up towards San Zeno. Then we take the road to Torri del Benaco and soak in the view of the lower section of the lake from next to the village church of San Martino in Albisano. This square is commonly known as the 'balcony of Garda' – and not without reason.

5:30pm: Back up North

From Torri, our route is straight up the Gardesana back to Torbole. The Vespa hire company doesn't shut until 8pm so we have enough time to enjoy the journey back.

7:30pm: Chitchat at the bar

After a pizza in Torbole we finish off our Vespa day with a Hugo cocktail, music and chatting to others in Wind's Bar (Via Matteotti 11).

❷ ★★ Malcesine & Monte Baldo

Why	Nobody really wants to miss the lake's most iconic landmark.
When	Early in the morning. It's not always the case – but in the high season in summer it can get pretty busy here just like in most of the other towns and villages around the lake.
Don't Miss	Fancy sketching the castle – just like Goethe did many moons ago? But, today, you certainly won't be arrested for spying as he nearly was.
Time	Plan at least one whole day: take the cable-car up Monte Baldo in the morning and stroll around Malcesine in the afternoon.
Tip	Perhaps you too will experience that 'magic moment'! (p. 78)

The red and ochre-coloured buildings and *palazzi* in Malcesine are closely grouped around the castle and harbour. A stroll through the twisty lanes reveals lots of delightful hidden corners and shady squares with cafés, a number of boutiques and souvenir shops. Monte Baldo towers above the town – the majestic massif stretches about 40km (25mi) down the eastern side of the lake as far as Torri del Benaco in the south.

Opposite page: Malcesine's Castello Scaligero sits on top of a rocky outcrop that drops down to the lake below

South of Torbole the *Gardesana Orientale* runs through the Riviera degli Olivi (Olive Riviera). In its early stages the road passes through several tunnels, but soon the silvery leaves of the trees can be seen shimmering on the hillside, seemingly mirroring the light bouncing off the waves on the lake. Ahead is Malcesine, the must-see on the eastern side of the lake, with the small Isola dell'Olivo out in the lake in front – just a short swim or easy row away.

Malcesine

The town is dominated by the Castello Scaligero dating from the 13th and 14th centuries. Much of the fortress is difficult to see unless you are on a boat. From the lake the genius of the construction is visible – a series of fortified walls surrounding three courtyards tumbling down a

rugged headland. The whole complex is now a museum and open to the public. On the left, after passing through the main entrance, is the *casermetta* (small barracks) of 1620 which now houses two little natural history museums focussing on the flora, geology and birds of Monte Baldo (Museo del Baldo) and the flora and fauna of Lake Garda (Museo del Garda). The balcony at the other end of the courtyard offers views of the mountains. Stairs lead up to the former gunpowder magazine which now houses the 'Goethe Chamber'. A copy of a drawing the German writer made while at the castle during his 'Italian Journey' – and which almost landed him in prison – is kept in the room. The Venetians took him to be an Austrian spy, sent out to reconnoitre military installations.

"On 3rd September [1786] at three in the morning, I slipped away from Carlsbad" The 'German Shakespeare', Johann Wolfgang von Goethe, spent nine months travelling around Italy. He later mentioned several times that this was the happiest time in his life.

Another set of steps leads through a portal to a third courtyard with a cistern (water reservoir) and a fresco of the Virgin Mary in the Late Byzantine style. A fishing museum (Museo della Pesca) is on the ground floor of the main building. Apart from exhibits related to fishing there are pictures of Venetian warships being heaved over the mountains to Lake Garda in 1435 and of attempts to salvage the man-of-war that sunk off Lazise. The upper storey and the tower can only be accessed by an external staircase. The masonry of the five-storey tower that was probably built by the Lombards, shows how far up the old tower reached. A window, now with bars, reveals where the drawbridge once was. From the platform at the top of the tower you can enjoy a splendid view over the town and across the lake.

The Corso Garibaldi leads right into the middle of the medieval Old Town. On the left is the Piazza Statuto, with the town hall on its eastern side. The lake and harbour lie just below the square. To the north there are lots of little alleys that open up into pretty squares with cafés, bars and shops. The castle, located higher up, is well signposted and reached via twisty little lanes. There is no lakeside promenade between the harbour and the castle but only side roads leading to the lake. Several cafés and restaurants however have terraces right on the water.

The crenelated Gothic Palazzo dei Capitani – which generally served as the governor's residence on the eastern

The Old Town of Malcesine clusters around the rocky ledge on which the fortress, towering above the narrow streets, is built. Goethe described Malcesine as "the first Venetian settlement on the eastern side of the lake".

side of the lake – is a reminder of Venetian rule (1405–1797). The entrance leads through a vestibule with a huge ceiling fresco depicting the castle, into a pretty little garden right on the lakeside. The tourist information office is in the left wing. The assembly hall (Sala delle Sedute), with a long Renaissance frieze and a slightly smaller audience chamber – also with frescos – now used for a variety of events, is on the upper floor.

A long promenade from the harbour leads southwards past the beach to a green promontory (45 mins.), the Val di Sogno (Valley of Dreams). Tiny Isola dell'Olivo juts out of the water just off the Lido Sopri and the privately-owned Isola del Sogno, a mere 5m (16ft) from the shore, can be seen from the bay of the Val di Sogno.

Magical Moment

Free as a Bird

Take to the air – float at ease like a feather! That doesn't have to remain a dream and is possible without any previous experience, too. But you really must have a head for heights. You must to be able to place your full confidence in the paraglider pilot and not tip the scales fully clad more than 110kg (245lb). Then off you go – from Monte Baldo, at an altitude of 1800m (5905ft)… *The tandem flight lasts a (magical) 30 minutes, depending on the thermals (www.tandempara gliding.eu).*

Monte Baldo

From Malcesine a cable-car will take you to the top of Monte Baldo, either to enjoy the view or for a walk along the ridge. Two parks have been set up to protect the plant and wildlife. The Riserva Naturale Integrale Lostoni Selva Pezzi has one boundary which follows the crest of Monte Baldo's ridge, the lower boundary running above the lakeside road. The second park, the Riserva Naturale Integrale Gardesana Orientale, is at the foot of the hill between Malcesine and Torbole.

The change in vegetation visible from the cable-car is remarkable. Close to the lake there are olive groves together with holm oak and Mediterranean pine. Higher up there are alpine species such as gentians, alpine orchids and plants such as *Lilium bulbiferum* and *Cyclamen purpurascens* or orange or tiger lily and purple cyclamen, while at the top of the ridge the species are those that would be expected on Arctic tundra rather than sun-soaked southern Europe – saxifrages and mountain avens, for example.

INSIDER TIP In Malcesine, the **Bar San Marco** in the hotel of the same name, located on the relatively new harbour, can be recommended. Even Goethe visited San Marco while touring Italy.

Spring on Monte Baldo: the view from here over the lake stretches for many miles.

187 D4

Museo Castello Scaligero
☎ 045 6 57 03 33
April–Oct daily 9:30–7;
Nov–March Sat, Sun 11–4 €6

Cable-car to Monte Baldo
April–Oct daily 8–6, Dez–March 8–4.
Every 30 mins., journey about 10 mins.
€15 (return: €20)

❸ ★★Garda

Why	The litle town that gave the lake its name is well worth a visit
When	Late afternoon – when you can watch the sun go down behind the hills on the other side of the lake
Don't Miss	Stroll around the town and treat yourself to a Hugo, Aperol or prosecco as the last rays of the sun shimmer on the water
Time	Half a day gives you enough time to see the most important things
Tip	Have you spotted the crocodile?

A crocodile? On Lake Garda? Yes, there is one – a very big one in fact. The foothills of Monte Luppia jut out into the lake right next to Garda and form a peninsula that, from the south, looks like the head of a huge crocodile. Garda has a remarkably mild climate as it is sheltered from the wind between the slopes of Monte Luppia to the north and the table mountain in the south with the ruins of a medieval castle perched on top.

The Nymph with Blue Hair

According to legend, the town and the lake got their name from the blue-haired nymph, Engardina who stole the heart

In Garda harbour – the perfect spot for a refreshing drink.

of a young water god. He made a big lake for her and, when she dived into it, the water turned the beautiful blue colour of her locks. As delightful as this tale may be, the name 'Garda' is most probably a corruption of the Alemanic *warden* meaning 'to observe' that, in turn, became *garden* – 'castle' in Old German.

Sheltered from the wind, between the northern slope of Monte Luppia and the table mountain to the south, Garda benefits from a pleasantly mild climate.

The remains of pile dwellings in the lake at the foot of the 'Rocca' and the ruins of a Celtic holy site on the mountain are evidence of the very early settlement of Garda. In the late 5th century, Theoderic the Great, King of the Ostrogoths, built a castle here. However, it was a woman in the 10th century who was to play a key role in the history of Garda and, in fact, of the whole of Italy. The Lombard Berengar I was living in the castle at this time and had his sights set on becoming king of Italy – but King Lothair I of Provence was in his way. It is highly likely that Berengar ordered him to be murdered and abducted Lothair's widow, Adelaide, in 951 and held her captive in the castle. Berengar was a tactical thinker. She should marry his son and strengthen his claim to the Italian throne. Adelaide refused and Berengar had her thrown into the dungeon. However, Adelaide managed to escape and became the wife of the Holy Roman Emperor Otto the Great who conquered Berengar and had him imprisoned for the rest of his life in Bamberg in Germany. Towards the end of the 13th century, Garda was ruled by the della Scala family; from the beginning of the 15th century it fell to Venice. Under Venetian rule the town blossomed but the castle was abandoned.

The town and 'Rocca'

The beautiful *palazzi* in the Old Town were built in the 15th/16th centuries under the Venetians. The Venetian Gothic Palazzo del Capitano is prominently positioned on the harbour. The water once lapped the base of the pale yellow building with its six lancet windows before the harbour basin was filled in and the Piazza Catullo with its

On the water-front in Garda: life can be a real treat…

cafés and *trattorias* extended. The master architect Michele Sanmicheli of Verona built the Palazzo Carlotti (also known as the Palazzo Losa) on the harbour too. The arcade on the ground floor of this Renaissance building is crowned by a loggia with five arches.

The principal thoroughfare, Corso V Emanuele, runs parallel to the lakeside promenade and becomes Via S. Stefano further south and then Corso XX Settembre with gateways to the town at each end. The Palazzo Fregoso was built in 1510 near the north gate.

The most most important building in Garda is at the northern end of the Old Town behind a high wall. The yellow section of the Villa Albertini is the oldest part dating from 1779. The red towers with their ornamental battlements where added in the 19th century. The King of Sardinia and Piedmont, Carlo Alberto, stayed in the Villa Albertini in Garda on 10 June 1848 from where the annexation of Lombardy to his kingdom was proclaimed following a plebiscite. The villa is privately owned and not open to the public.

A walk to the ruins of the Rocca on the 300m (985ft)-high hill to the southeast of the town takes just under an hour and offers a wonderful view of the lake. Sturdy shoes are recommended. Turn left next to the church of Santa Maria Maggiore (15th century, later remodelled in the Baroque style) into Via S. Bernardo that bends right after just a few yards. The Via degli Alpini will be seen on the right that then leads up the hill.

There is a good market the length of the *lungolago* every Friday morning

INSIDER TIP Have a cup of coffee or sample the ice cream in **Giardinetto** on the lungolago (no. 27).

 186 C2

❺ ★★Riva del Garda

Don't Miss	One of the biggest and best-known holiday centres in the region
Why	For this very reason (see above). And because there is really a lot to see here: a moated castle, a leaning tower…
When	Mornings, when the sun is shining: from round about four in the afternoon Riva is generally no longer in the sun
Time	Half a day at least but you can easily spend much more time here, as you wish
What Else	Strolling around and 'seeing and being seen', as well as…
Tip	…shopping: Riva has a number of lovely boutiques

The elegant town that is one of the biggest and best-known holiday resorts in the area has one of the most important harbours on the lake as well as a beautiful Old Town. While many a beach on Lake Garda is no wider than a towel, the beach in RIva is so big that it is seldom jammed packed even in high season in August. There are lots of trees that provide shade and access to the beach is free of charge.

Riva is on the northwest of Lake Garda and is flanked by two mountains. To the east it is separated from neighbouring Torbole by Monte Brione that is a mere 376m (1233ft) high.

The palazzi built in the Lombard-Venctian style (the Palazzo Municipale can be seen on the right) and the arcades in Riva reflect the influence of Verona.

To the west, the rocky foothills of Monte Rocchetta (1521m/4990ft) rise steeply above the town. Its strategically favourable location that enabled it to take control of the trade route crossing the Alps on a north/south route and extending as far as the Po plain, made it much coveted – first by the Princely-Bishops of Trentino, then by the Counts of Arco, the Scaliger family from Verona, the Viscontis of Milan and the Venetians. The decisive maritime battle fought between the Venetians and the Milanese, that resulted in the Venetians gaining control of the whole of the Lake Garda region, took place off Riva in 1438. After the Congress of Vienna, Riva fell to Austria in 1875 and remained under Austrian rule until 1918. Around 1900 the town was a popular destination for aristocrats and the upper class as well as for artists and writers. Franz Kafka, Thomas Mann, Friedrich Nietzsche, Rainer Maria Rilke, Sigmund Freud and D. H. Lawrence are just some of the famous who spent some time here.

Old Town

Friedrich Nietzsche was so taken by the leaning clock tower, the Torre Apponale on Piazza Tre Novembre, that he said that he would like to live there as a hermit at the end of his life

The Piazza Tre Novembre on the harbour lies at the centre of the Old Town. Of all the brightly painted buildings with their long arcades, an ensemble of three grand *palazzi* on the west side – which now includes the town hall – stands out in particular. The Palazzo Pretorio and the Palazzo del Provveditore on a corner site both date from the 14th century and were built by Cansignorio della Scala. The Palazzo Municipale where the Venetian governor resided was added in the 15th century. An arcade and a castelated town gateway (Porta Bruciata) lead to the little Piazza Rocco. The open apse of the former church of San Rocco can be seen on the right. On the eastern side of the square is the slightly leaning 34m (112ft)-high Torre Apponale which was built as a fortification and integrated in the town wall in the 13th century. The Rocca to the east of the Torre Apponale is surrounded by green on a little island with a moat. It was erected by the Scaligers in 1124 and later remodelled by the Austrians who used it as a barracks. It houses the Museo Alto Garda with its display of archaeological finds from the region and a collection of paintings from the 16th to the 20th centuries.

A stroll around the Old Town should also include a visit to the 'Church of the Holy Virgin', Riva's most important art-historical building. Built in the early 17th century by an unknown Portuguese architect, the Chiesa dell'Inviolata has an elaborate Baroque, octagonal interior – all gilding and plasterwork.

Bird's eye view: Riva del Garda with the Piazza Tre Novembre on the harbour; on the east side is the Torre Apponale that was built in the 13th century.

Surrounding area

One of two exquisitely beautiful ships, the paddle steamer 'Zanardelli' that dates from 1903, operates exclusively in the north around Riva, Limone, Malcesine and Torbole. Its counterpart, the 'Italia', plies the south. The fastest direct link between Riva and Peschiera takes 3½ hours. A round trip of the whole lake taking in all the most important places can only be done in one day if you go without visiting the individual places en route (www.navigazionelaghi.it).

Some 200m above the town, a round tower sticks out above the treetops on the slopes of Monte Rocchetta. It is the last remnant of a Venetian fortress destroyed by the French in 1703. It offers wonderful views over the town and the lake.

From Riva take the 421 – towards Lago di Tenno – for 4km (2mi) to reach Varone where the Cascata del Varone plunges 90m (294ft) into a narrow gorge. Walkways have been constructed to allow you to get close and admire their power and experience the noise and spray.

INSIDER TIP Riva has one of the most beautiful promenades on the lake. Sit at a table here or in **Caffè Città** on the Piazza Tre Novembre and soak up the atmosphere.

---

181 D5

Museo Alto Garda (MAG) & Torre Apponale (Rocca di RivaTorre)
0464 57 38 69 www.museoaltogarda.it June–Sep daily 10–6; March–May, Oct, Nov closed Mon
Museum €5, tower €2

Cascata del Varone
0464 52 14 21
May–Aug daily 9–7; April, Sep 9–6; March, Oct 9–5, Nov–Feb Sun and public holidays only 10–5
€5.50

At Your Leisure

22 San Martino della Battaglia & Solferino

The decisive struggle for Italian unification against the Austrian Empire and the Habsburgs, the Battle of Solferino, was fought on 24 June 1859. The appalling suffering of wounded soldiers, left to die an agonising death on the battlefield without medical help, led to the founding of the Red Cross by the Swiss humanist and devout Christian Henri Dunant.

On a clear day, the 65m (213ft)-high tower at San Martino can be seen from Lake Garda. A 400m-long ramp spirals upwards culminating in a viewing platform. The walls on the ramp are covered in paintings of the Italian war of independence. The Museo della Battaglia just a few yards beyond has displays of uniforms and memorabilia from the war in 1859.

186 B1
Torre di San Martino e Museo
030 9 91 03 70
March–Oct daily 9–12:30, 2:30–7, Nov–Feb 9–12:30, 2–5 €5

Museo Della Croce Rossa
Via Garibaldi 50, 46044 Castiglione delle Stiviere 0376 63 85 05
www.micr.it April–Oct 9–noon, 3–6, Nov–March 9–noon, 2–5 €5

23 Parco Giardino Sigurta

About 8km (5mi) south of Peschiera, near Valeggio sul Mincio, is the 60ha (148 acre) Parco Giardino Sigurta, the work of Count Carlo Sigurtà (1898–1983). Using water from the River Mincio, for which the count had secured the rights, he transformed the dry, hilly, moraine landscape into one of the most beautiful landscaped gardens in Europe. Sigurtà devoted himself to tending the park for almost 40 years; it was then taken over by his nephew, Enzo. The park has been open to the public since 1978.

186 C1 045 6 37 10 33
March–Oct daily 9–7; Nov 9–6 €12

24 Peschiera del Garda

Peschiera, where the River Mincio leads out of Lake Garda, has always been strategically important. It was occupied by the Romans and, in medieval times, there was a castle and a walled harbour. When the Austrians held the area they demolished the castle but reinforced the walls, making Peschiera one corner of their defensive quadrilateral, the other corners being Legnago, Mantova and Verona. The Austrian defences remain and are still uncompromising, although overgrown. They can best be seen from a boat. In the main square look for the town hall clock with the beaks of two bronze eagles striking the hour.

186 C1

25 Gardaland

Gardaland, just north of Peschiera, is Italy's biggest and most popular theme park. New features are added each year so that those who keep coming back time and again will not get bored at all. It is safe to say that if you have children and they like roller-coasters, water rides, fantasy characters, dolphins, safaris, play areas and much, much more, they will love Gardaland. The park caters for children from 'just walking' upwards and there are plenty of refreshments. Sealife and the Delfinarium also belong to Gardaland. At weekends in summer a free shuttle tram runs the 2km (1.2mi) from the station in Peschiera to Gardaland. At this time of year, both the park and the car parks in particular are generally full to bursting.

186 C2 ☎ 045 6 44 97 77
www.gardaland.it
Easter, June–Sep daily 9–11; 9–6 rest of the year From €30

26 Lazise

An intact town wall surrounds the historical centre of Lazise. As this is a traffic-free zone you can stroll around the pretty lanes with their shops, cafés, *trattorias* and restaurants at your leisure. In the Middle Ages the Roman settlement of Lasitium rose to become a market town with a castle. The Scaligers rebuilt the fortress in the 13th century and gave it the appearance it still has today with castellated towers and a walkway along the battlements. Under Venetian rule it became a place of key importance. Today, the Scaliger castle is lived in and, together with the Villa Bernini, surrounded by a park (not open to the public). The centre, the imposing Piazza Vittorio Emanuele with its beautiful chequerboard paving, surrounded by a row of pretty houses with restaurants and *trattorias*, leads to the narrow harbour basin. The two wide arches of the Arsenal (Vecchia Dogana) from the 14th century open towards both the harbour and the lake. The building of random white stone and pebbles served as a customs house, among other things. Today, it is used for temporary exhibitions. The slender belltower of the church of San Nicolò (12th century), which is decorated with beautiful frescos, rises behind the Arsenal.

186 C2

Piazza Vittorio Emanuele, Lazise

Federica who, together with her brother and sister Fausto and Elena, now runs the Zeni wine-growing estate in Bardolino that has been in family ownership since 1870, knows what makes a good wine.

27 Bardolino

Among the best known wine-growing areas around the shores of the lake is the region around Bardolino where the red wine of the same name is pressed. There is a museum of wine in the town and you can follow a route through the wine growing area. But Bardolino does not turn its back on olives and one of the exhibits at the the Museo dell'Olio d'Oliva is a hydraulically driven olive press from the 19th century.

The Piazza Matteotti – actually more a wide promenade than a square – with its many shops, cafés and *trattorias*, forms the heart of the Old Town. The entrance to the Neo-Classicistic church of Santi Nicolò e Severo is flanked by four tall columns (19th century). Open-air concerts given by the Bardolino Philharmonic Orchestra are held weekly between June and September with the church as a backdrop.

A dilapidated tower on the lakeside promenade is all that remains of the Scaligeri fortress. Lovely walks are to be had from the lakeside promenade: to the north as far as Garda (3km/1.8mi), passing olive groves, bathing areas and small clumps of trees en route and, to the south to Cisano. San Severo, with its tall slender *campanile*, is one of the most beautiful and best preserved Romanesque churches in the area around Verona. The layout of the random stone building that dates from the end of the 11th century is not symmetrical – the length and width of the side aisles are different. Inside, the walls are covered with unusually vibrant frescos. One of the oldest buildings from the Carolingian period is the small church of San Zeno, tucked away in the Via San Zeno. The tiny, narrow single-aisled building that seems unusually high was constructed in the 8th century to a cruciform plan. At the end of the Borgo Cavour is the grand, privately-owned villa of the local, long-established Guerrieri Rizzardi family. It lies in a large park laid out in the 16th century that stretches down to the lakeside promenade. Wine and oil produced on the estate is sold in a shop next to the gate.

186 D2
Museo del Vino
Via Costabella 9 045 7 21 00
www.zeni.it daily 9–12:30, 2:30–7
Free, 'aroma gallery' with wine tasting and finger food (charge made)

'Museo dell'Olio d'Oliva
Via Peschiera 54, Cisano
045 6 22 90 47 www.museum.it
March to mid-Jan daily 9–12:30 and Mon–Sat 2:30–7 Free

28 Punta di San Vigilio

The Romans were obviously captivated by the charm of this promontory covered in meadows, olive groves and cypress trees that lies 3km (1.8mi) to the west of Garda, as they built a villa here. The privately-owned Villa Guarienti now occupies the site at the end of an avenue of cypresses. Laurence Olivier and Winston Churchill stayed in the luxurious hotel Locanda di San Vigilio which has just 14 rooms. A church dedicated to a 13th-century hermit, San Vigilio, a private marina and an exclusive restaurant are also located here. Anyone wanting to swim around the Punta may do so from the spotless Baia delle Sirene (Bay of the Sirens) which also boasts a restaurant, showers and a children's play area.

186 C2
Public bathing area
Parco Baia delle Sirene
June–Sept Mon–Sat 9:30am–8pm, Sun 9am–8pm €12

Punta di San Vigilio: one of the most beautiful spots on Lake Garda

Lega delle Bisse: rowing competition in traditional boats that are rather like Venetian gondolas.

29 Torri del Benaco

Another Scaligeri castle, still attached to a section of the Old Town walls, guards the headland that overlooks the eastern terminus of the car ferry. The imposing castle is now a museum documenting industries from local olive oil and lemon production to lake fishing and quarrying – Torri del Benaco was once well-known for its reddish-yellow marble, used for many buildings in Verona, for example.

There is also a collection of prehistoric rock engravings from the area.

The old lemon-trading house, Lemonaia, built in 1760, can also be visited: the building is one of few that now survive from the time when lemons were as important as olives to the economy around Lake Garda.

The church of Santa Trinità with 14th-century frescoes in the style of Giotto is well worth a visit. The *chiesa* is situated on the pretty, old harbour at the heart of Torri del Benaco, overlooked by the castle built to protect it.

186 C3
Museo del Castello Scaligero di Torri del Benaco and Lemonaia
☎ 045 6 29 61 11 www.museodelcastellodi torridelbenaco.it June–Sep daily 9:30–1, 4:30–7:30; April–May and Oct 9:30–12:30, 2:30–6 €4

30 Nago-Torbole

While, generally speaking, only a few tourists a year find their way to Nago, a village located some 150m

(492ft) up on a rocky plateau above Torbole, thousands stream to the beach below in summer. Torbole sits snugly on the shore of the lake and has become one of the most important centres for surfing and sailing on Lake Garda. Mountain bikers and climbers find ideal conditions here too as the north of Lake Garda is almost entirely enclosed by mountains with well signposted hiking trails and climbing routes. The only noteworthy sight in Nago is the ruined fort (13th century) that once guarded the Val d'Adige area down to Lake Garda. The strategically sited fort was owned in turn by the Counts of Arco, the Castelbarco family, the province of Trentino and the Venetians, before it was slighted by the French in 1703. Today, it houses a good restaurant serving specialities from Trentino.

187 D5

31 Arco

To the north of Lake Garda, some 6km (3.7mi) from Riva and Nago-Torbole, is the steep-side Arco mountain with its castle. At its foot is the pristine climatic health resort with avenues of palm trees, beautifully renovated Renaissance buildings and pretty shops. The mild climate of this little town was the reason why the Habsburg Archduke Albrecht of Austria chose to move to his winter residence here from 1872 onwards. Nowadays Arco attracts freeclimbers in particular. Every year in September the 'Rock Master' world championships are held in Arco. The arboretum in Arco (Arboreto), originally the park surrounding the archducal palace, has miniature landscaped areas focussing on the native countries of various plants.

187 D5

Castello di Arco
Via Castello 04 64 51 01 56
April–Sep daily 10–7; shorter opening hours at other times €4

Parco Arciducale Arboreto
Via Lomego 04 64 58 36 36
April–Sep 8–7; Oct–March 94 Free

Climbing in Massone near Arco.

Where to... Stay

Expect to pay per double room, per night
€ under €80
€€ €80–€150
€€€ over €150

BARDOLINO

Aqualux €€
One of the best spa hotels on the lake with eight pools and seven saunas, located on the outskirts of the town.
186 C2 Via Europa Unita 24
045 6 22 99 99 www.aqualuxhotel.com

Hotel du Lac et Bellevue €€€
90 rooms and suites, restaurant, bar, pool, sauna, gym and jetty.
186 C2 Via Santa Cristina
045 6 21 03 55
www.hotel-du-lac-et-bellevue-bardolino.it

GARDA

Locanda San Vigilio €€€
A grand address in an exquisite position on Punta San Vigilio; good and (very) expensive.
186 C2 Punta San Vigilio
045 7 25 66 88 www.punta-sanvigilio.it

LAZISE

Principe di Lazise €€
Pretty country hotel on the edge of the town in a hilly area rather like Tuscany. Two pool, four saunas and very good spa facilities. Highly recommendable restaurant.
186 C2 Località La Greghe
045 6 49 01 77
www.hotelprincipedilazise.com

MALCESINE

Hotel Aurora €
Hotel with contemporary but comfortable rooms at the heart of Malcesine. Friendly staff. Car Park.
187 D4 Piazza Vittorio Emanuele 10
045 7 40 01 14
www.aurora-malcesine.com

Guesthouse Grand View €€€
The name is a bit of an understatement! This pretty guesthouse is more of a modern B&B – and the vista can only be described as *grandissima*. About 3km (1¾mi) above Malcesine.
187 D4 Località Masotta
045 6 59 02 19
www.guesthousegrandview.com

Villa Monica €€
Good 3-star hotel, located on one of the most beautiful beaches on the lake.
187 D4 Località Baitone 045 6 57 01 11
www.villamonica.com

PESCHIERA DEL GARDA

Hotel Ristorante Bel Sito €
Ideally positioned for excursions to local attractions and Verona. 2-star hotel with swimming pool, garden and tennis court; bike hire available.
186 C1 Via Venezia 62 045 6 40 09 21
www.belsitohotel.com

RIVA DEL GARDA

Du Lac et du Parc €€€
Particularly lovely 4-star hotel with its own spa in the middle of beautiful grounds that run down to the lakeside.
187 D5 Viale Rovereto 44
0464 02 18 99 www.dulacetduparc.com

Lido Palace €€€
This exclusive 5-star hotel is a perfect blend of traditional and contemporary styles and one of the best hotels on the lake. Very good restaurant, very elegant spa.
187D5 Via Carducci 10
04 64 02 18 99
www.lido-palace.it

TORRI DEL BENACO

Baia dei Pini €€€
The villa is right on the beach, furnished in a modern but rather idiosyncratic style. Pool and car park.
186 C3 Via Gardesana 115
045 7 22 52 15 www.baiadeipini.com

Where to... Eat and Drink

Expect to pay for a three-course meal for one, excluding drinks and service
€ under €30
€€ €30–€50
€€€ over €50

BARDOLINO

Trattoria Da Nanni €€€
Well worth the short trip inland to Costermano: Claudio Mazzurana's home cooking is excellent.
186 C2 Via Gazzoli 1, Costermano
0457 20 00 80 www.dananni.com
Closed Tue for lunch, Mon

BRENZONE

Belvedere €
This family-run restaurant offers regional specialities such as rabbit, homemade noodles and pizza baked in a wood-fired oven. Excellent selection of *grappa*.
187 D4 Località Marniga
045 7 42 00 55 Closed Tue

GARDA

Bussola Garda €
The owner makes the pasta, for a main course the crayfish is to be recommended. There is a garden for *al fresco* dining.
186 C2 Via Spagna 29 045 7 25 64 75
www.labussolagarda.com
Closed Nov–March

Trattoria Al Graspo €€
'I am the menu', says the chef and owner, Luca. A meal of several course can be had at a (fair) set price.
186 C2 Piazza Calderini 12
045 7 25 60 46 www.graspo.it
Closed Nov–March

LAZISE

Alla Grotta €€
On the old harbour opposite the Venetian Customs House. Fish specialities change on a daily basis (as do the few meat dishes) – raw and cooked, fresh from the lake or brought in from the sea.
187 D5 Via F. Fontana 8
045 7 58 00 35
www.allagrotta.it/en/index.html
Closed Tue, and Dec–Jan

Corte Olivo €€
In the summer the tables are in a lovely inner courtyard inside the Old Town walls. Traditional menu.
187 D5 Corso Cangrande 22
045 7 58 13 47 Closed Tue

Osteria Valesana €
Almost everything is grilled – the *grigliata mista* is difficult to better! Homemade *bigoli* with a white *ragù*.
187 D5 Via San Martino, 69, Corte Valesana 345 4 60 81 74
www.cortevalesana.it
Daily in summer

MALCESINE

Vecchia Malcesine €€€
The menu in this Michelin-starred restaurant includes fish from the lake (try the poached pike); few meat dishes.
187 D4 Via Pisort 6 045 7 40 04 69
www.vecchiamalcesine.com
Closed Wed, Feb and lunch Nov–Jan and March

PESCHIERA DEL GARDA

La Torretta €€
Eat in a fine old building with wooden beams in the heart of old Peschiera – or sit outside under the sun umbrellas.
186 C1 Via G Galilei 12
045 7 55 01 08 Closed Wed

RIVA DEL GARDA

Mediterraneo €€
Pleasant restaurant serving traditional Italian meals and pizzas cooked in a charcoal stove.
187 D5 Piazza Garibaldi 6
0464 55 01 75 Closed Tue

You can't get fresher than this! Alberto Rania is one of the last professional fishermen on Lake Garda. What he catches early in the morning is sold on the Piazza Battisti in Riva on Tue, Fri and Sat from 10am onwards.

Where to... Shop

There are markets in Bardolino (Thu, antiques market on every 3rd Sun), Brenzone (Tue); Garda (Fri); Lazise (Sat); Malcesine (Sat); Peschiera del Garda (Mon); Riva del Garda (June–Sept on every 2nd and 4th Wed, Oct–May every 2nd Wed); Torbole (every 2nd and 4th Tue); Torri del Benaco (Mon)

BARDOLINO

In the countryside inland from Bardolino, in Cavaion Veronese, is the Serene winery that offers exellent prosecco and red wines; only available from the producer and at a very reasonable price for such quality (Località Sorsei 5, www.serenewine.com).

GARDA

For leather goods go to Mola (Corso Vittorio Emanuele 36). Beautiful jewellery can be found at Modini (Corso Vittorio Emanuele 26). For art, Garda Ceramiche (Via A. Manzoni 20) has excellent ceramics.

LAZISE

For ceramics, try Il Gatto Nero (Corso Ospedale 29). Antico Mulino alla Torre (Via Raffaello 35) stocks Italian crafts, jewellery, soaps and basketry, while Clacson (Corso Ospedale 28) has lovely children's clothes.

MALCESINE

Millenium Pelletteria (Piazza Statuto 18) has a good selection of leatherware. For jewellery try Voglia d'Oro (Via Capitanato 1). There are few art outlets in town. Onice (Corso Garibaldi 53) which specialises in ceramics. For a good selection of lace, candles, oils and gifts head for Casanova (Vicolo di Mezzo 5).

PESCHIERA DEL GARDA

It is worth having a peek in Più Gioielli (Via Rocca 21) for jewellery and silverware. Giulia sells high-quality perfumes in her shop Parfum Idéal (Via Rocca 23): the petals, spices and tobacco from which the perfumes are made, are soaked in oil for up to six months to give them their unique scents. Candela d'Arte Giesse (Piazza Betteloni 14) has handmade candles.

RIVA DEL GARDA

For something different try Fronte Lago (Viale San Francesco 9) which has weird but wonderful bags and scarves. For jewellery head for Easy Gold (Via Santa Maria 3), Orafo (Via Monatanara 16) that specialises in gold, or Re Artu Bijoux (Via Lipella) which has ultra-modern jewellery.

TORBOLE

Coast to Coast (Via Matteotti 10) is good for young women's fashions; Gioielleria Santoni (Via Matteotti 13) has lovely jewellery. Surfing equipment and accessories are very much in demand. The legendary Point-7 Store Torbole is a little way out of town at Via Sabbioni 15 and always has the very latest for the surfing scene.

Where to... Go Out

SPORT AND LEISURE

Watersports
There is a large number of windsurfing, kiteboarding and sailing schools at the northern end of the lake. For windsurfing, the best schools are Sailing du Lac (at Hotel du Lac et du Parc, tel: 04 64 55 24 53) in Riva del Garda and Circolo Surf (tel: 04 64 50 53 85), Conca d'Oro Windsurf (tel: 04 64 54 81 92), Surfcenter Lido Blu (at Hotel Lido Blu, tel: 04 64 50 63 49) and Surf Segnana (at Hotel Paradiso, tel: 04 64 50 59 63) in Torbole. The Stickl Sportcamp is run by the former surfing world champion, Heinz Stickl (Via Gardesana 144 in Val di Sogno di Malcesine, tel: 045 7 40 16 97, www.stickl.com).
For sailing contact Heinz Stickl (above) in Malcesine, Fraglia Vela Riva (tel: 04 64 55 24 60), Lega Navale Italiana (tel: 04 64 55 52 01) or Gardaseecharter (tel: 33 55 27 45 54) in Riva, or Circolo Vela (tel: 04 64 50 62 40).
There is a diving school at Riva – Gruppo Sommozzatori, at Porto S Nicolò (tel: 04 64 55 51 20).
Canoe tuition/hire is available from Canoa Club Canottieri Riva (tel: 04 64 55 52 94).

Adventure Sports
Several organisations for rock climbing, canyoning and paragliding are available, i. e. Kletterschule Franz Heiss in Nago (tel: 3466 12 01 99), Canyon Adventures (tel: 3348 69 86 66) in Torbole oder Fly 2 Fun (tel: 3349 46 97 57) in Malcesine.

Golf
The 18-hole Club Paradiso del Garda at Peschiera del Garda (tel: 03 65 91 35 40) is the only course on the eastern shore.

FESTIVALS

There is a festival of medieval games in Lazise in June.
Wine festivals are held in June in Peschiera. Peschiera also has a palio in August in which boats with single or double pairs of oars race along the town's canals.
The Young Musicians' Festival is held at the end of July in Riva. Malcesine has a series of music evenings during the summer.
However, the most important festival takes place at the end of September/beginning of October in Bardolino. Some 100,000 visitors flock to the traditional wine festival that has been held since 1929. Young wines and tasty dishes can be sampled and the spectacular closing fireworks display enjoyed.

NIGHTLIFE

At the northern end of Lake Garda, the nightlife is a bit meagre, with the exception of Riva where you can find hip bars such as the Riva Bar (Largo Medaglie d'Oro 2), with a wide range of gins distilled locally on Lake Garda, the Maracaibo (Via Monte Oro 14, also a disco), and No Name (Piazza Catena 15). Bars and pubs: Pub all'Oca (Via Santa Maria 9) and Pub Lochness (Viale Dante 39).
Fully-fledged discos can be found inland in Arco. In Torbole, the Wind's Bar (Via Matteotti 11) is the hotspot for surfers and surfing tips.
Summer evenings are always loud, long and lively at the Beach Bar Vaca Loca (Via Gardesana 9) in Assenza di Brenzone.

Verona's Piazza Bra, the 'city's living room', unites 2000 years of history and a contemporary savoir-vivre to form of a highly atmospheric complete work of art.

Verona

What would Verona be without Romeo and Juliet? One thing is certain – it would still be an incredibly beautiful city...

Pages 96–123

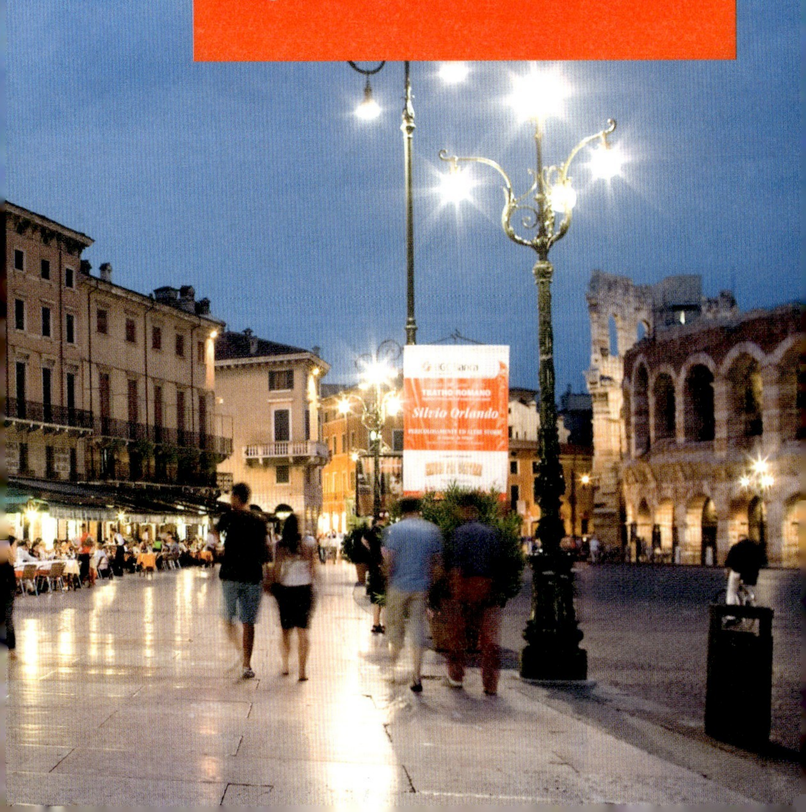

Getting Your Bearings

Verona, the capital of the province of the same name, is located on a bend in the River Adige, with ten bridges linking it to districts on the other bank. Its historical centre is listed as a UNESCO World Heritage site.

It was already an important site under the Romans from 89BC onwards. It was here, at the end of the strategically important Brenner mountain pass, that three Roman roads converged: the Via Claudia, connecting the north, as well as the routes east and west – the Via Postumia and the Via Gallia. The most famous building in the city, the Arena, also dates from the Roman era. After the Romans had created their chequerboard ground plan in a bend on the Adige river and constructed a town of considerable strength, the Goths occupied the site. Theoderic the Great made Verona the royal city of the Migration Period around the year 500.

From the mid 13th century it was ruled by the princely house of della Scala from Milan (also written as Scaligeri or Scaliger). In 1405 the city came under the rule of Venice for a period of some 400 years. In 1797 Verona and Venetia became Austrian and, when Austria lost Venetia to Italy, the city was incorporated into the Kingdom of Italy in 1866.

TOP 10

❻ ★★ Piazza Bra & Arena di Verona

❼ ★★ Piazza dei Signori

❽ ★★ Piazza delle Erbe

Don't Miss

32 San Zeno Maggiore

At Your Leisure

33 Castelvecchio & Ponte Scaligero

34 Tomba di Giulietta

35 San Fermo Maggiore

36 Casa di Giulietta

37 Santa Maria Antica

38 Sant'Anastasia

39 Duomo

40 Museo Archeologico & Teatro Romano

41 Giardini Giusti

42 San Giorgio in Braida

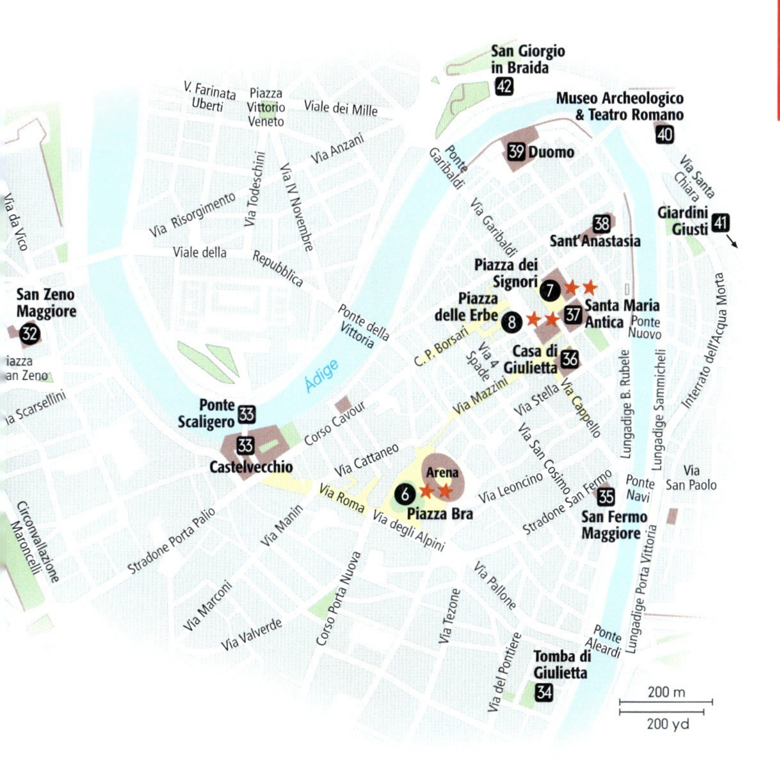

My Day on the Trail of Romeo and Juliet

“It was the nightingale and not the lark...” So here we are, in the city where the world’s most famous love story is supposed to have unravelled. That may have been a little while back, but the tragic fate of Romeo and Juliet can be felt everywhere even to this day. It’s well worthwhile tracing the steps of this drama about two unfortunate lovers.

10am: It’s all Shakespeare’s Fault

Let’s start on the ❻ ★★ Piazza Bra, a world famous little square with the magnificent Arena as a backdrop. A bronze bust of William Shakespeare can be found in the archway in the southwestern corner of the *piazza*. He’s the one responsible for the whole Romeo and Juliet hype! Thank-you – O Bard of old!

10.30am: Tender Kisses

Just before reaching the Casa di Romeo nibble a ‘Juliet kiss’. The Pasticceria De Rossi (Corso Porta Borsari 1a) sells *baci di Giulietta*, a sweet temptation made of marzipan and icing. Delicious! We wander off in the direction of Romeo’s house, crossing the ‘city’s belly’ – the Piazza delle Erbe.

10.45am: “O Romeo!”

The brick-built townhouse dating from the Middle Ages with a tower and crenellated defence wall recalls how powerful and wealthy Romeo’s family was. The residence is privately owned and

1pm: "Dost Thou Love Me?"
10:30am: Tender Kisses
Posta di Giulietta
10:45am: "O Romeo!"
Osteria Giulietta e Romeo
1pm
C. St. Anastasia
7
Casa di Romeo
10:30am
8
10:45am
11:15am: "O Woe!"
C. P. Borsari
Pasticceria de Rossi
10am: It's all Shakespeare's Fault
36
Via Cappello
11:15am
Via Giuseppe Mazzini
Via Oberdan
2:30pm
Start/ End
Arena di Verona
10am/ 9pm
Via Roma
6
Portoni de la Bra
2:30pm: Time for shopping
Via degli Alpini
Via Pallone
100 m
100 yd
9pm: "A Thousand Times Good Night!"
5:30pm: "And all My Fortunes at thy Foot I'll Lay"
Via del Pontiere
34
5:30pm

Top: Off we go – the Piazza Bra is a popular spot in the morning not only for Romeos and Juliets. Right: Pledges of eternal love are repeatedly made at the Casa di Giulietta.

the interior is not open to the public. Romeo's family, the Montecchis, were Ghibellines who supported the Holy Roman Emperor, whereas Juliet's family, the Cappellettis, were adherents of the Guelphs and supported the Pope. A constellation that would seem to make the love between Juliet and Romeo an impossiblity.

11.15am: "O Woe!"

A crowd of people clusters around the gateway to Via Cappello outside the 36 Casa di Giulietta. To the left and the right messages of love are scribbled on the walls. Lots of kisses or pledges of eternal love are given here. The bronze statue of Juliet has only been here since 1972. Her right bosom has been polished after years of being groped so unashamedly by almost every visitor. For the superstitious, 'love remains a dainty thing' to anyone who does this. The balcony actually dates from the 13th century, as does Juliet's house, but originally no balcony existed. Shakespeare invented it, like most of the things in the tragic love story that takes place in the 14th century. You can find out more about Romeo and Juliet, the most important moments during their tragic romance and historical facts in the museum here.

1pm: "Dost Thou Love Me?"

The way to a man's heart is famously through his stomach: that's why we head for a (good) restaurant for lunch with an (even better) sound-

Above: From Verona with love. An evening visit to a performance in the Arena is the perfect way to round off the day.

ing name – the Osteria Giulietta e Romeo. How about *pasta e fagioli* – noodles with white beans? A dish typical of Verona and very tasty, too! The small restaurant can be found at no. 27, Corso Sant' Anastasia.

2.30pm: Time for Shopping

Now we need our credit card. And who can resist a stroll around the shops when here? The Via Mazzini, the main shopping street, is just a few minutes walk from the *osteria*.

5.30pm: "And all My Fortunes at thy Foot I'll Lay"

The world needs love... even if it leads to death! So off we head to what is popularly known as Juliet's grave: the 34 Tomba di Giulietta, in the catacomb of the church of San Francesco. You can even get married here today.

9pm: "A Thousand Times Good Night!"

Having rested, changed and after eating a little snack in the early evening, we're now ready to attend a performance in the 6 ★★ Arena di Verona. If it's not '*Aida*' then it could be '*Carmen*', another drama about love and power.

Romeo and Juliet-themed guided tour:
A guided tour with a difference is with one of the many 'Juliets' who answer the up to 7000 letters sent every year to 'Julia, Verona, Italia'. One such guide is Manuela Uber (tel: 347 4717404, manuela.uber@gmail.com; a guided tour for up to 25 participants costs €115 and lasts around 2½ hours).

6 ★★ Piazza Bra & Arena di Verona

Why	Because of the Arena, the opera festival, Shakespeare
When	Always. But it is that much better in the summer combined with a visit to the opera
Don't Miss	Sing and let sing
Time	One day and one night (with the opera)
Tip	People-watching on Piazza Bra...

It's best to start a tour of the city at the Piazza Bra which, with the Arena di Verona in the middle, is one of the most visited squares.

Piazza Bra

The *piazza* is entered from the south through the Portoni della Bra, a twin-arched gateway with a tower that was added around 1400 by the Viscontis. *Palazzi* with frescos, arched windows and pretty balconies (16th–18th century) enclose the square which is lined with cafés and restaurants. The south side is marked by the Gran Guardia Nuova (Palazzo Municipale), the city hall built between 1835 and 1843 with a semi-circular extension added after 1945. Next to this is the elongated former Gran Guardia, a Venetian building with a huge loggia (1614).

In the evening on the Piazza Bra: people strolling around the Arena and along the wide paved area

The Teatro Filarmonico concert hall (1716) and the Museo Lapidario Maffeiano are behind this. The scholar Scipione Maffei (1675–1755) of Verona had the latter built for his collection of Ancient Greek and Roman sculptures, sarcophagi, reliefs and much more.

Backstage during the opera festival: a costume designer dresses Giancarlo Frison, a member of the choir, for his role as a soldier in Bizet's opera 'Carmen'.

Arena di Verona

The two-storey row of arcades that gives us the picture we have today of the Roman amphitheatre, built in the 1st century AD for gladiator and bull fights, was originally surrounded by another, three-storey outer wall of red Veronese marble. Only four arcades of the once magnificent façade now remain on the north side. The interior comprises an elliptical area (138m × 109m/453ft × 358ft) with 45 tiers and seating for 15,000. In 1913, to mark the 100th anniversary of Giuseppe Verdi's birth, an opera festival was held in the Arena for the first time. This now takes place every year between June and September.

A production of Verdi's *Aida* involves more than 700 people, from handworkers, technicians and lighting engineers to scene-shifters, wardrobe attendants and production managers.

The Piazzetta Mura Gallieno, rather like a courtyard behind the amphitheatre, is used for storing props for the various different operas performed during the festival season. On change-over days, cranes are used to heave the huge stage sets into or out of the Arena. You may even see the Sphinx fly...

INSIDER TIP **Bar Liston** at no. 12 is excellent for coffee while the **Olivo** at no. 18 is good for lunch.

189 D3

Museo Lapidarium Maffeiano
045 59 00 87
https://museomaffeiano.commune.verona
Tue–Sun 8:30–2 €4.50

Arena
045 8 00 32 04 www.arena.it
Mon 1:30–7:30, Tue–Sun 8:30–7:30. During the opera season the Arena closes at 3:30pm €10

Music instead of fights

The Roman amphitheatre is a theatre of perfect proportions and its size is testimony to Verona's historical importance.

1 Oval: The actual arena is a hollowed-out oval at the centre of the round building. This was where gladiator and bull fights as well as animal baiting took place. It measures almost 74m (242ft) long and 45m (148ft) wide.

❷ Cavea: The spectator area is made of tiered stones each 45cm (18in) high. This area provides seating for up to 15,000 people. The external length of the elliptical plan, measured from the main entrance, is 138.8m (455ft).

❸ Basement: Technical equipment now occupies the basement area of the amphitheatre. This was where there were originally rooms for the gladiators and cages for the animals.

❹ Velaria: The spectator area can be roofed over by an arrangement of awnings.

❺ Ala: The outer façade of the Arena was originally clad in stone. This was almost completely destroyed in an earthquake in 1183. Only one section at the northern end has survived and reveals the building's original height.

❻ Façade: The arches along the present façade were originally part of the building's interior. As can be seen, the reddish marble has been effected by exposure to the elements.

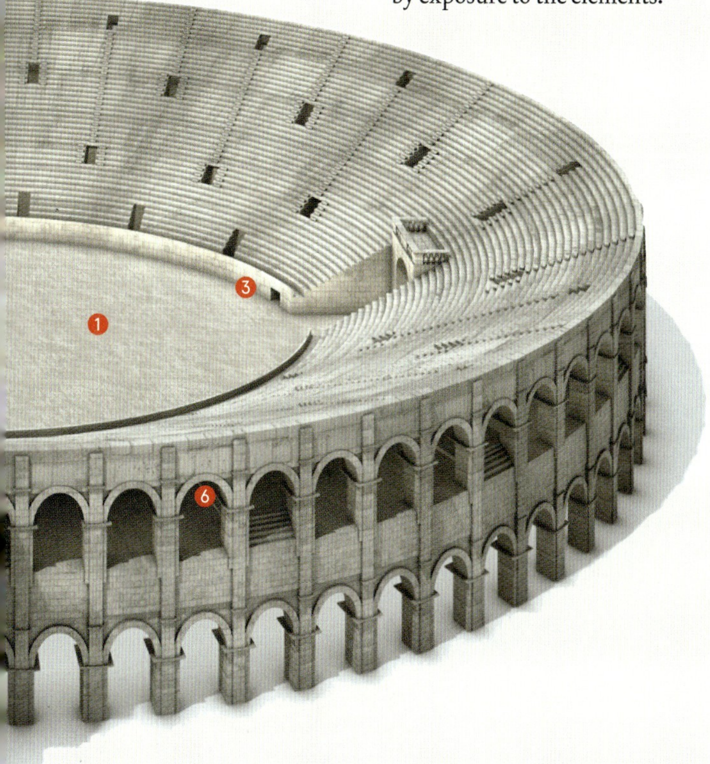

7 ★★ Piazza dei Signori

Why	Because it is one of the most elegant squares in the whole of northern Italy
When	As early as possible, even before the shops have opened
Don't Miss	About half a day
Time	Watching and soaking up the atmosphere – while drinking an espresso
Tip	Musing over Dante's words: "Perceive ye not that we are worms, designed to form the angelic butterfly."

The Piazza dei Signori, once Verona's administrative district and the seat of the government, is the city's elegant 'drawing room' surrounded by magnificent town palaces.

Five large, richly decorated arches span the points where neighbouring streets join the square and link the stately buildings with one another. Coming from the Piazza delle Erbe, you enter the square below the mighty walls of the Palazzo del Comune. An external marble staircase (c. 1450) that was once roofed over, leads up to the former Council Chamber from the inner courtyard surrounded by a row of tall arcades. The Torre dei Lamberti towers above the building.

An intimate square to relax: the Piazza dei Signori.

In 1575 an arch was added over the narrow Via Dante to create an optical link between the Palazzo Comunale and the Palazzo dei Tribunali. The fortress-like, quadrangular building and the defence tower were erected by the much-feared Cansignorio della Scala. The structure was later used as an artillery school and the seat of the Venetian governor. The loggia dates from 1476; the Renaissance portal was created in 1530 by Michele Sanmicheli. One of the most beautiful Early Renaissance buildings is the two-storey Loggia del Consiglio on the north side of the *piazza* (1486–1493). The building is crowned by five statues of famous people from Ancient Verona. The castellated Palazzo del Governo closes off the eastern side of the square. It was also a residence of the della Scala family. Giotto and Altichiero decorated the palace with frescos, of which only sections have survived to this day.

After being expelled from Florence, Dante Alighieri lived in Verona for around seven years – in 1303/1304 and again from 1312 until 1318. A monument dedicated to him can be seen in the centre of the square.

The Scaliger in Verona

For 110 years, between 1277 and 1387, the Ghibelline noble family della Scala ruled over the city. By entering into tactical pacts with the lagoon city of Venice, allowing Venice access to Verona's markets and transport routes, Mastino I della Scala succeeded in ensuring the city's economic boom. His brother, Alberto della Scala, got rid of all his opponents, thus securing his family's continued rule. The most influential member of the family was Cangrande I della Scala (1291–1329), who called poets and scholars to his court, including Dante. Under his rule, the city republic expanded into a territorial state, absorbing Vicenza, Feltre, Belluno, Padua and Treviso. The final decades of dynastic rule, however, were marked by intrigue and torture, culminating in a startling series of murders within the family until the Scaligeri had virtually annihilated themselves. This paved the way for the no less brutal Viscontis of Milan.

INSIDER TIP If you are just looking for a bite to eat or a cup of coffee head for the bar and restaurant in **Caffè Dante** (no. 2) housed in a Renaissance building from around 1500 that has now been beautifully restored.

189 E4

8 ★★ Piazza delle Erbe

Why	Things are always busy on the central market square
When	Climb the Torre dei Lamberti as soon as it opens at 9am
Time	Around half a day
Don't Miss	The same applies here too: people-watching while drinking an espresso

The Piazza delle Erbe, one of Italy's most beautiful squares, lies at the heart of the Old Town and hosts a flower and vegetable market on weekdays.

Opposite page: The Madonna Verona with a scroll in her hand dominates the market fountain on the Piazza delle Erbe. The scroll bears the inscription: 'For this city, the upholder of justice and beloved of praise.'

This was originally the site of the forum in the Roman city. It now lies 4m (13ft) below the present ground level. The Capitello, a pedestal crowned by a canopy (16th century), from where important decisions and court rulings were proclaimed, is located on the square. Further to the north is the market fountain. Merchants used to gather in the Casa dei Mercanti opposite the Palazzo del Comune that was constructed in 1301 and rebuilt in 1878.

North of the Palazzo del Comune are the Case dei Mazzanti behind the passage onto the Piazza dei Signori. The beautiful Renaissance frescos on the façades were commissioned by the Mazzanti family that acquired the buildings in 1517.

The Baroque Palazzo Maffei (1668) on the north side of the square houses the tourist information office. Nearby is the Torre del Gardello which boasts the oldest town clock in Verona dating from 1370. A wonderful panoramic view of the square can be had from the 84m (276ft)-high Torre dei Lamberti on the other side. A lift whisks visitors to the top from the inner courtyard of the Palazzo del Comune.

INSIDER TIP The **Mezzaparte** at no. 8a serves the best hot chocolate – and coffee of course!

189 E4

Torre dei Lamberti
☎ 045 9 27 30 27 Dialy 9–7 €8

PIAZZA DELLE ERBE

32 San Zeno Maggiore

Why	One of the most beautiful Romanesque churches in northern Italy
When	At 8.30am, when it first opens
Time	Two hous are probably enough
Don't Miss	Enjoy the magnificent works of art and the meditative peace

The large Basilica San Zeno Maggiore, one of the most beautiful Romanesque churches in northern Italy, is flanked by a belltower and a castellated defence tower. The present building was erected in the 12th century over the tomb of the city's patron saint, Zeno, as the church of a Benedictine monastery.

Zeno was Bishop of Verona from 362 until 371. He originally came from Africa which explains why the Gothic seated figure in the burial church of San Zeno is made of black marble. He was one of the major Early Christian pulpit orators who vehemently defended the teachings of Christ in Veneto in the face of the rapid spread of paganism. Medieval legends praise the care he showed for the poor and the sick as well as his unrelenting work to ward off Arianism, the followers of which do not consider Christ and God to be coessential but

View of the basilica's central aisle. The Romanesque elements in the interior of the church dedicated to the patron saint are monumental but refined at the same time

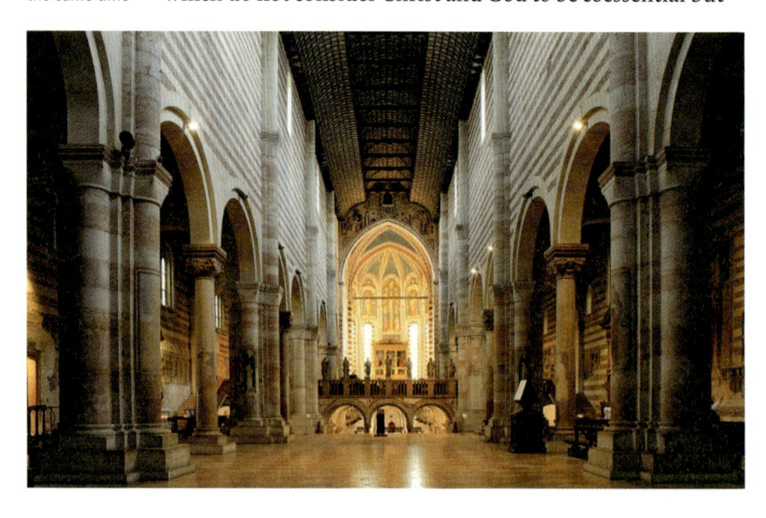

solely similar in nature. When Zeno died on 12 April 371, he left an extensive collection of interpretations of the scriptures in Latin as well as treatises on baptism, the Easter liturgy and Mariology.

The west façade is dominated by a large rose window and a portal made by Master Nicolò, a magnum opus of Gothic sculptural art. It is shielded by a projecting baldachin whose columns rest on two stone lions. In the tympanum over the portal, Bishop Zeno hands the banner of the free commune to the people of Verona. The famous bronze doors have a wooden core to which the bronze panels were nailed. Stylistic differences show that they were created in two phases. In the scenes depicted on the older panels created around 1100, there is no spatial depth and the figures are not supported on a base; in the later reliefs (c. 1200), a feeling of space is created through the use of perspective. The panels show scenes from the Old and the New Testaments, miracles performed by St Zeno, figures of kings and allegories of virtues. The high central nave has an unusual wooden ceiling (14th century) whereas the raised choir has ribbed vaulting. The crypt, laid out like a large lower church, is under the choir. 48 columns with artistically worked capitals support the vaulted ceiling. A balustrade with statues of Christ and the Apostles (*c.* 1260) separates the nave from the choir where the most important work of art in the basilica can be seen – a three-part altarpiece with the Virgin Mary in the centre, an early work (1456–1459) by the major Renaissance painter Andrea Mantegna. The painting in the church is however a copy. The glowing colours and the impression given of a three-dimensional pictorial space that is continued in the architectural features framing the scene, are characteristic of Mantegna's masterly painting.

The cloister, built in 1123, can be reached from the northern side nave. The vaulted ceiling was altered in the style of the period in the 14th century. The cloister is dominated by an imposing Romanesque campanile.

INSIDER TIP A good place for lunch is the **Trattoria Al Calmiere** on Piazza San Zeno, a little bit further away, which has a lovely terrace where you can sit in the shade.

---

188 B4
March–Oct Mon–Sat 8:30–6, Sun 12:30–6;
Nov–Feb Mon–Sat 10–1, 1:30–5, Sun 12:30–5

At Your Leisure

33 Castelvecchio & Ponte Scaligero

The complex on the banks of the Adige, built in the mid 14th century under Cangrande I, comprises two sections – a fortress and barracks facing the city that was to protect the Scaligers more from the Veronese than other enemies, and a palace with the living quarters. Between the two there is a tall defence tower through which you pass to get to the Ponte Scaligero. The wide-arched bridge, completed in 1375 to enable the inhabitants of the Castelvecchio to flee across the Adige in the face of danger, is castellated and has bastions and defence walkways. After the fall of the last Scaliger in 1387, the fortress complex fell into ruin. It was restored in 1923–64 and now houses the Museo di Castelvecchio. At this time the former defence tower was given a Venetian-Gothic façade. The historical rooms inside the art museum were designed by the architect, Carlo Scarpa. An impressive collection of artworks by Veronese sculptors and painters from the 12th to the 18th centuries is shown in 29 rooms. Sculptures from the 12th to the 15th centuries are exhibited in the first rooms, followed by examples of Veronese painting (14th/15th centuries), including *Madonna of the Quail* by Pisanello. Other exceptional works from the heyday of Veronese Gothic and Renaissance painting, such as by Turone and Bellini, are also to be seen. Important paintings by Veronese, Tintoretto and Tiepolo, for example, document the 16th and 17th centuries. One of the most important works of art in the museum is on a plinth between the defence tract and the residential wing, namely the ambiguously smiling knight, Cangrande della Scala, on horseback (14th century).

Ponte Scaligero, Verona's most beautiful bridge.

Museo di Castelvecchio
188 C3 ☎ 045 8 06 26 11 11
museodicastelvecchio.comune.verona.it Tue–Sun 8:30–7:30, Mon 1:30–7:30 €6

34 Tomba di Giulietta

Close to the river in Via del Pontieri, about 350m south of the Arena, is the Tomba di Giulietta, a 14th-century marble sarcophagus, now empty, which tradition has it was the last resting place of Shakespeare's heroine. Legend also says that Romeo and Juliet were married in the Franciscan monastery that once stood here, but there is no more truth in this than in the legend linking Juliet with the sarcophagus in the Baroque chapel. But as with Juliet's House, the site feels right and that feeling is shared by the many who come here to drop love letters in the sarcophagus or coins in the courtyard fountain. Far removed from the realm of fiction, the medieval frescos in the small Museo degli Affreschi adjoining, have their very own stories to tell.

Tomba di Giulietta/ Museo degli Affreschi
189 E2 ✉ Via del Pontiere 5
☎ 045 8 00 03 61
🌐 museodegliaffreschi.comune.verona.it
🕐 Mon 1:30–7:30, Tue–Sun 8:30–7:30
€4.50

35 San Fermo Maggiore

North of Juliet's tomb, in a square at the town end of the Ponte Navi, stands the Church of San Fermo Maggiore. Between 1065 and 1138 Benedictine monks built a church on top of an older building from the 6th century that was dedicated to the two Veronese martyrs Fermo and Rustico (†361). The Franciscans who were granted the church in 1260 changed the three-aisled upper church into a hall church and extended it to the west. To the east, the remarkable choir group was created that is characterised by the contrasting Gothic main choir with its towering lancet windows and the four small Romanesque apses. A tour of the Gothic upper church (13th/14th centuries) is recommended before entering the Romanesque lower church (11th/12th centuries). The sculptures, wooden ceiling and the frescos in the upper church are outstanding. By contrast, the lower church is a simple, dignified, vaulted structure. Here too there are some good frescos.

189 F3

36 Casa di Giulietta

Year in, year out, some three million people make their way to Verona to see for themselves the city in which William Shakespeare placed what is probably the most famous love story in literature. It is possible that the writer had heard the Italian saying – attributed to Giordano Bruno: "*Se non*

Casa di Giulietta is said to bring good fortune in matters of the heart

è vero, è (molto) ben trovato" (If it is not true, it is (certainly) well conceived). At any rate, Verona makes a good living from Shakespeare's play and, to give the fictive story a real location, Antonio Avena – the director of Verona's museums at the beginning of the 20th century – had a balcony made from a sarcophagus in the museum depot and added it to the house of the Cappello family. The name of this dynasty of merchants from the 13th century is remotely reminiscent of Juliet's family, the Capuletis. The Gothic window and the portal with its pointed arch were also taken from other buildings and so the stage set was completed. Two roads further north, in the Via Arche Scaligere, is the 'Casa di Romeo' – a remnant of a former town palace belonging to the Montecchi (Montague) family.

189 E4 Via Capello 23
045 8 03 43 03 museodegliaffreschi.comune.verona.it Daily 9–7 €8

37 Santa Maria Antica

The passage between the Palazzo del Governo and the Palazzo dei Tribunali leads from the Piazza dei Signori to the small, three-aisled church of Santa Maria Antica (12th century), the Scaliger's private church. Above the portal is the sarcophagus of Cangrande I (†1329), borne by two dogs that are a play on the ruler's name – Cangrande, meaning 'large dog'. A copy of an unusual statue of a laughing equestrian figure (the original is in Castelvecchio) can be seen over the baldachin above the tomb. The Gothic tombs of other members of the della Scala are in the family cemetery next to the church (Arche Scaligere). The cemetery itself boasts the sarcophagus of Mastinos I (†1351) and the magnificent, exquisitely fashioned tomb of Cansignorio (†1375). Both have richly decorated baldachins with pyramidal roofs, crowned by equestrian figures of the respective Scaligers. The artistically worked railings around the cemetery are from the 14th century.

189 F4

38 Sant'Anastasia

The church of Sant'Anastasia, close to the bank of the River Adige, is also reached from the Piazza dei Signori down a narrow alleyway. This mighty brick building – the largest Gothic church in Verona – was the Dominican monastery church. It was started in 1290 but not completed until 1481. From the other side of the Adige, you can get a good view not only of the delicately balanced architecture of the bell tower but also of the choir section with its six polygonal chapels. The overall impression one has of the dark interior, divided into three aisles by tall columns, is dictated by the coloured floor, the red marble pillars and the ornamental painting of the cupola. The two stoups (holy water fonts) on the first pair of columns are sup-

View from Castel San Pietro of the Adige and Verona's city centre

ported by hunched figures called the 'due gobbi'. The figure on the left is from 1500 and is attributed to Caliari, the father of the famous artist Paolo Veronese. The figure on the right is nine years older. The tomb of the *condottiere* Cortesia Serego of 1429, a field marshal under the Scaligers, is in the main choir. The chapels to the left and right of the main choir have excellent Late Gothic frescos. The southernmost chapel is especially interesting as a superb votive fresco by Altichiero dating from around 1390 embellishes the wall surrounding the tomb of Federico Cavalli. The fresco *St George and the Princess*, that Pisanello painted around 1435 above the arch to the first chapel on the right of the main entrance, is considered a masterpiece of Upper Italian painting, in which the Late Gothic style is not only perfected but, at the same time, superseded. This can readily be seen in the depiction of the horse where the extreme, foreshortened perspective already hints at the spatial feeling found in Renaissance painting.

189 F4

39 Duomo di Santa Maria Matricolare

Externally, Verona's cathedral is a Romanesque basilica. The ornamental work is concentrated primarily around the main portal that is considered to be the work of Maestro Nicolò. In addition to prophets, two figures of warriors can be seen on the columns to the side of the portal. These are reputedly Roland and Olivier, two *paladine* (peers) in Charlemagne's court. The monumental interior, subdivided by groups of columns into three aisles of almost equal height, is characterised by later modifications, especially those of the 15th and early 16th centuries. Among the most impressive works of art inside the cathedral is the large-format altarpiece in the first chapel on the north aisle which includes one version of Titian's painting *The Assumption* (c. 1540).

> ✈ 189 E5
> ☎ 045 59 28 13 ● March–Oct Mon–Sat 10–5:30; Nov–Feb Tue–Sat 10–5, Sun and public holidays 1:30–5 🎟 €2.50

40 Museo Archeologico & Teatro Romano

On the other side of the Ponte della Pietra – one of two Roman bridges in the city – the rows of seats in the former Roman theatre, dating from the time of Emperor Augustus (63BC–14AD), climb the slope below the Castel San Pietro. In summer the theatre is used for concerts, ballet performances and plays. The church of Santi Siro e Libera (10th century) with its Baroque marble steps and late medieval San Girolamo monastery are located above the seating area. The monastery now houses the archaeological museum (Museo Archeologico).

> ✈ 189 F5 ✉ Via Redentore 2
> ☎ 045 8 00 03 60
> 🌐 www.museoarcheologico.commune.verona.it ● Tue–Sun 8:30–7:30, Mon from 1:45 🎟 €4.50

41 Giardino Giusti

The Porta Organa leads to the Palazzo Giusti (1580). The adjoining Renaissance garden is a little paradise. Beyond a hedge maze with statues peeking over the tops and the sound of bubbling water features, the park stretches up the slope, interspersed with narrow paths that pass through grottoes and old pavilions. On the hillside there is a more natural area following a re-design in the 19th century. The cypresses are such a feature of this section that Goethe is said to have picked some twigs from them as a souvenir.

> ✈ 189 off F5
> ✉ Via Giardino Giusti 2
> ☎ 045 8 03 40 29 ● April–Sept daily 9–8; Oct–March daily 9–7 🎟 €7

42 San Giorgio in Braida

If, instead of turning right at the end of the Ponte Pietra, you bear left beside the river you will reach the domed church of San Giorgio in Braida. Built in the 15th century on the site of an earlier church, the prominent dome was added by Sanmicheli 200 years later. Inside there are a number of fine artworks, including what many believe to be Paolo Veronese's masterpiece, *The Martyrdom of St George*, and a *Baptism of Christ* by Jacopo Tintoretto.

> ✈ 189 E5

Seeking Refuge in a Green Oasis

Verona is not Rome. But Verona isn't a little village either. When strolling around the city, doing a bit of sightseeing and shopping, you might like to have a short rest in a little oasis in the city centre after a cup of coffee. This place in Verona is called the Giardini Giusti – a beautiful Renaissance garden with tall cypress trees and statues of gods and goddesses such as Adonis, Apollo, Diana, Juno and Venus. It is the perfect place to step back in time into the world of mythology and to enjoy a magical moment in peace and quiet.

Where to... Stay

Expect to pay per double room, per night
€ under €80
€€ €80–€150
€€€ over €150

Hotel Accademia €€€
Right at the heart of the historic centre, the Accademia is just a short walk from Juliet's House. It occupies a 17th-century *palazzo* and combines antique furnishings with modern facilities. Well appointed rooms and an excellent restaurant.
189 E3 Via Scala 12 ☎ 045 59 62 22
www.hotelaccademiaverona.it

Bologna €€
In a lovely, fully renovated, old building in a quiet area just a 50m walk from the Arena. Well-appointed rooms, friendly staff and secure parking.
189 D3 Piazzetta Scalette Rubiani 3
☎ 045 8 00 68 30
www.hotelbologna.vr.it

De Capuleti €€
Best-Western-Hotel, close to Juliet's tomb and so about 10 minutes' walk from the Arena. It has been modernised to a high standard.
189 E2 Via del Pontiere 26
☎ 045 8 00 01 54
www.hotelcapuleti.it

Due Torri Hotel €€€
A 13th-century *palazzo* close to the church of Sant'Anastasia is Verona's most exclusive hotel. The public rooms with their arches and stylish bedrooms are the height of elegance and every possible convenience is provided. The restaurant is, as would be expected, first class.
189 F4 Piazza Sant'Anastasia 4
☎ 045 59 50 44
hotelduetorri.duetorrihotels.com

Giulietta e Romeo €€
Pretty little hotel right behind the Arena. From here, everything can be reached on foot. Or, if you prefer, you can borrow a bicycle free of charge. Please note: the rooms are very small.
189 E3 Vicolo Tre Marchetti 3
☎ 045 8 00 35 54
www.giuliettaeromeo.com

Grand Hotel €€€
The Grand is very well positioned on the road linking the city centre with the A4 *autostrada* and is just a few minutes' walk from the Piazza Bra. Very modern rooms and a delightful private courtyard garden.
189 D2 Corso Porta Nuova 105
☎ 045 59 56 00 www.grandhotel.vr.it

San Marco €€€
Close to San Zeno Maggiore and so a 20-minute walk, or short bus ride, from the main centre. Breakfast is served in the garden. There is also a pool and saunas.
189 off A3 Via Longhena 42
☎ 045 56 90 11 www.sanmarco.vr.it

Verona €€
Well-appointed rooms and tastefully furnished public areas on the edge of the Old Town. Perhaps a little too cool but stylishly modern nonetheless.
189 D2 Corso Porta Nuova 47/49
☎ 045 59 59 44 www.hotelverona.it

Verona Mi Piace €
Some 2km (1.25mi) from the city centre, this simple bed & breakfast has just 3 rooms and makes a pleasant place to stay in expensive Verona for those on a tighter budget.
188 off A5 Via Angelo Emo 10
☎ 393 8 11 03 84
www.bedandbreakfast.eu/bed-and-breakfast/verona/verna-mi-piace/2562670/

Hotel Veronesi La Torre €€€
This prettily renovated former monastery is a few miles from the centre. Tip: for those visiting during the festival season there are often rooms still to be had here. Lovely spa with sauna, pool and jacuzzi.
187 D1 Via Monte Baldo 22, Dossobuono di Villafranca ☎ 045 8 60 48 11
www.hotelveronesilatorre.it

Where to... Eat and Drink

Expect to pay for a three-course meal for one, excluding drinks and service
€ under €30
€€ €30–€50
€€€ over €50

Al Capitan della Cittadella €€€

This fish restaurant is not cheap but the food is in a class of its own.
189 D2 Piazza Cittadella 7
045 59 51 57 www.alcapitan.it
Closed Sun, Mon

Al Cristo €€

Close to the Ponte Nuovo and so a little distance from the city centre, this restored 16th-century *palazzo* is worth the walk. Try the *spaghetti allo scoglio* served with a mass of fresh seafood...
189 F4 Piazzetta Peschiera 6
045 59 42 87
www.ristorantealcristo.it
Closed Mon

Antica Bottega del Vino €€

Tucked away off the Via Mazzini, the Antica Bottega del Vino is wonderfully atmospheric with its bottle-lined walls. Specialities include the chef's tortellini, polenta dishes and horse meat. The wine list runs to about 100 pages. The service is superb.
189 E3 Via Scudo di Francia 3
045 8 0045 35
www.bottegavini.it
Daily 11am–1am

Arche €€

A characterful *trattoria*, the menu comprises traditional dishes with a modern twist. The steamed turbot fillet on a bed of spinach in a ginger sauce is delicious.
189 E4 Via Arche Scaligere 6
045 8 00 74 15 www.ristorantearche.com
Closed Sun (dinner) and Mon

La Costa in Bra €

La Costa claims to be the oldest pizzeria in town – the first pizza oven was installed here in 1962. The non-pizza menu is limited, but excellent. Good service and in summer you can eat *alfresco*.
189 D3 Piazza Bra 2
045 59 74 68 www.lacostainbra.it
Daily 9–midnight

Il Desco €€€

The best 2-star cuisine in a wonderfully atmospheric setting. A fantastic place with prices to match. The (9-course) tasting menu costs €150.
189 F3 Via Dietro San Sebastiano 7
045 59 53 58 Closed Sun and Mon

12 Apostoli €€

Giorgio Gioco is not just an excellent chef but is also known as a writer of poems in the local Veronese dialect. The interior is rather like a film set. Near the Piazza Erbe.
189 E4 Corticella San Marco 3
045 59 69 99 www.12apostoli.com
Closed Sun (dinner) and Mon

Greppia €€

Close to Via Cappello and Piazza Erbe in a quiet square. Veronese dishes such as *baccalà with polenta*.
189 E4 Vicolo Samaritana 3c
045 8 00 45 77
www.ristorantegreppia.it
Closed Mon

Mondodoro €

Fine old *osteria* just off Via Mazzini offering year-round al fresco dining. Veronese menu and local wines.
183 E4 Via Mondo d'Oro 4
045 8 94 92 90 www.osteriamondodoro.verona.it Closed Mon

Where to... Shop

VIA MAZZINI

For general shopping, the best place is Via Mazzini and the nearby streets. Via Mazzini itself is home to Gucci, Versace, Max Mara, Marinarinaldi, Bulgari and Cartier, among others. But there are many less internationally famous brands that are worth visiting too. For young fashions try Promod, Pimkie and Oltre. For shoes and bags look at Rossetti, Bruschi and Furla.
Erbovoglio is excellent for children's clothes and shoes.
Al Duca d'Aosta has high-quality clothes and shoes for both men and women.
A huge range of leather goods can be found at Campana, with everything from wallets to luggage.
Jewellery can be found at Damiani (no. 59).
Fiorucci and Upim, Verona's biggest department stores, are also in Via Mazzini (no. 6 and no. 10).

LEATHER

As well as the Via Mazzini shops try Principe (Corso Porta Borsari 31) or Folli Follie (shoes and bags at no. 42). There is also Bettanin & Venturi (Vicolo Morette 4) where shoes have been made for almost 150 years.

FASHION

Corso Porta Borsari has many elegant fashion shops such as Carlo Bottico, Just Cavalli, Burani and Stizzoli for classically elegant ladies' fashions, while Dismero, Patrizia Pepe and iam design for a younger, trendier clientele. For something more avant garde, go to Lazzari (Piazza Erbe 15). Class Country (Via San Rochetto 6) has traditional menswear, as does Class Uomo at no. 13b in the same street. Camicissima (Piazza Bra 3) has a large range of inexpensive men's shirts.

GALLERIA RIVOLI

The passage near the Piazza Bra has several shops including Antiqua for antiques, Giancarlo for shoes and bags, La Dispensa Mamma Pia for wine and olive oil and Nereo Stevanella for elegant silver jewellery.

ANTIQUES

The best area for antiques is Corso Sant'Anastasia and the adjacent streets. There are also good shops closer to the *duomo*. However, be cautious, as there is a thriving trade in reproductions.

JEWELLERY

Apart from Damiani (see Via Mazzini) it is also worth visiting G&G Amighini (Piazetta Monte 3), which specialises in silver.

MARKETS

There is a daily market on the Piazza Erbe. There are also markets on the Piazza San Zeno on Tuesdays and Fridays, on the Piazza Isolo on Tuesdays and on the Piazza Santa Toscana on Wednesdays and Fridays.

Every third Saturday of the month there are antiques, objets d'art and crafts on the Piazza San Zeno.

OUT OF TOWN

North of Verona, in the Centro Commerciale in Affi, is a warehouse outlet selling a wide range of Italian clothing and footwear.

Where to... Go Out

CARNIVAL

Verona carnival is one of the oldest in Italy, dating back to the early 16th century. It is held in the early spring. The highlight of the event is the last Friday before Shrove Tuesday, known as the *Bacanal del Gnoco*, at which the Papa del Gnoco, holding a huge potato dumpling on a fork, takes charge. Contact www.tourism.verona.it for exact dates.

FESTIVALS

There is an International Film Festival in the city in April. From June to August there are Shakespearean plays (performed in Italian) in the Roman amphitheatre.
At Christmas the Festa di Santa Lucia is held, with seasonal street markets on the Piazza Bra and Via Roma. The Piazza Bra celebrations include displays of cribs from around the world in the arcades of the Arena.
The Opera Festival held in the Arena from mid June until the beginning of September is world famous. Book ahead (tel: 045 8 00 51 51) to be sure of a ticket. 'Real' fans tend to go for the – cheaper – tiered seats, where they can follow the text in the light of a little reading lamp and even join in the singing of the best-known arias, sometimes at a considerable volume.

THEATRE

As well as the Roman amphitheatre there are several other theatres in the city.
The Teatro Nuovo has a famous drama festival from December to April, whereas operas are staged at the Teatro Filarmonico from February to April.

NIGHTLIFE

The Veronese have their own version of a British 'pub-crawl' – *andar per goti*, 'do the Goth Walk'. There are, consequently, a large number of bars, many of them with live music, particularly at weekends. For the best, head for the Piazza Bra or Piazza Erbe.
The city is surprisingly short of discos and nightclubs. Popular at the moment are Dorian Gray, a stylish disco at Via Belobono 13, the Atlantis Pub (Piazza Cittadella 7) with regular live music and Alter Ego (Via Torricelle).
There are, however, several out-of-town nightspots. Berfei's Club is a disco/restaurant (Via Lussemburgo 1) off the road towards the A4 *autostrada* (Verona South exit).
Alternatively, try Night City Club (Via Bresciana 1f) which is located off the SS11 Verona–Peschiera road.

HITS FOR KIDS

The Arena offers the possibility of treading ground once trodden by gladiators and Castelvecchio and its weaponry also appeals to most children.
Areas around the city's old defensive walls have been made into parks and two of these have good children's playgrounds – Arsenale near Castelvecchio and Raggio di Sole near Porta Nuovo.
The La Spiaggia@Village, close to Bussolengo, northwest of Verona, has a vast swimming pool with rock towers and other 'natural' features, and a roller-skating rink. Although it is not specifically aimed at children, most will enjoy it.
The Parco Natura Viva, a combination of a safari park and a zoo with over 250 wild species and 1500 creatures in all, is also in Bussolengo and incorporates a dinosaur park with life-sized models.

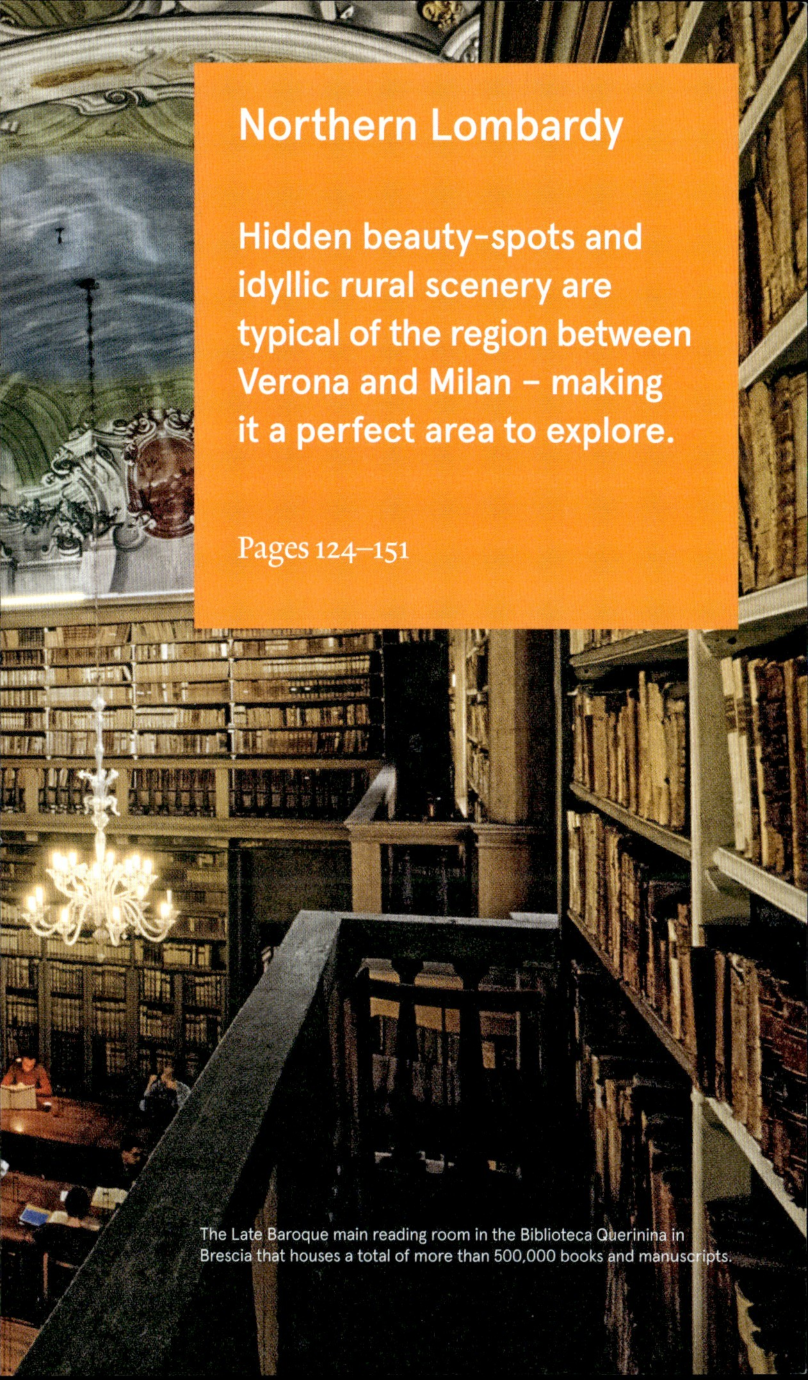

Northern Lombardy

Hidden beauty-spots and idyllic rural scenery are typical of the region between Verona and Milan – making it a perfect area to explore.

Pages 124–151

The Late Baroque main reading room in the Biblioteca Querinina in Brescia that houses a total of more than 500,000 books and manuscripts.

Getting Your Bearings

To this day Bergamo and Brescia have remained important centres at the point where old trade routes cross and the southern Alps run into the plain of the River Po. Their enchanting Old Towns have many historical relics dating from Antiquity up to the heyday of the Venetian Republic. The area around Lago d'Iseo is picturesque. Val Camonica is a UNESCO World Heritage site famous for its rock drawings.

Brescia is Lombardy's second largest city after Milan, a prosperous place with interesting Roman remains, some good Renaissance buildings and a museum housing some of the finest art-historical treasures in Italy. Visitors, however, first have to pass through less attractive industrial areas and cope with the permanent traffic jams that plague the outskirts of the city until they can get closer to the real sights in the historic city centre.

Bergamo is a city with two totally different faces. On the plain is the sprawling Città Bassa, the busy lower town of modern buildings and industry. On a ridge, some 120m above the River Serio, is the Città Alta, the medieval upper town with a labyrinth of narrow alleyways and lots of art treasures.

North of Bergamo and Brescia beautiful valleys cut into the Alpine foothills; to the east is Val Camonica, with a renowned thermal spa and fascinating prehistoric drawings in the Parco Nazionale delle Incisioni Rupestri.

TOP 10

9 ★★ Bergamo

10 ★★ Lago d'Iseo

Don't Miss

43 Brescia

At Your Leisure

44 Boario Terme

45 Breno

46 Capo di Ponte

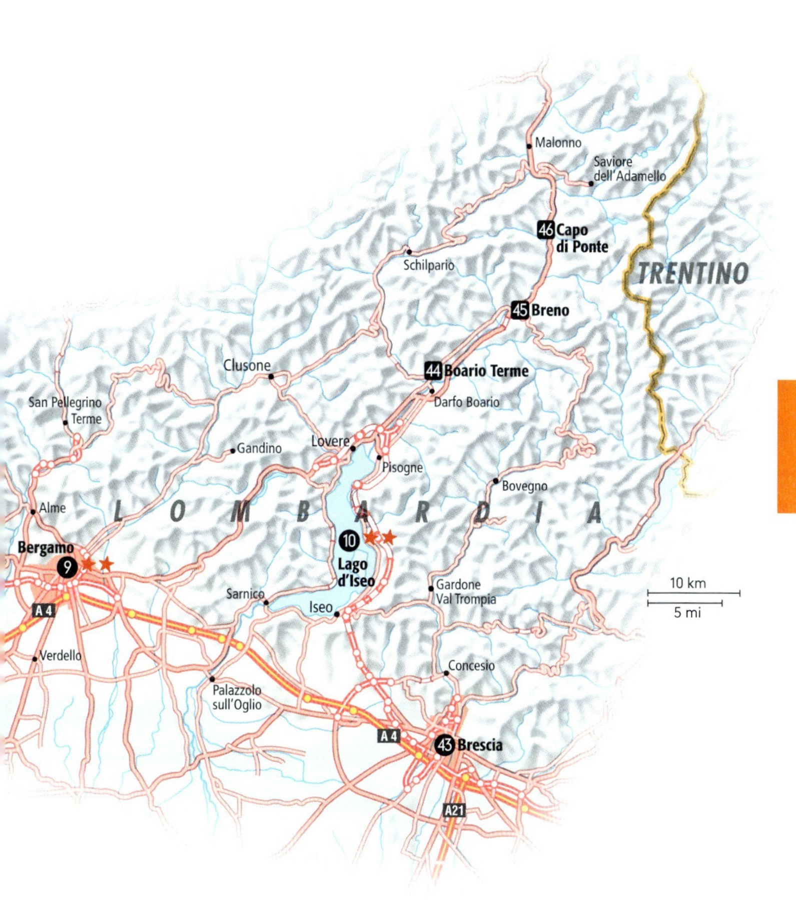
Malonno
Saviore dell'Adamello
46 Capo di Ponte
Schilpario
TRENTINO
45 Breno
Clusone
44 Boario Terme
San Pellegrino Terme
Darfo Boario
Gandino
Lovere
Pisogne
Bovegno
Alme
L O M B A R D I A
Bergamo
9
10
Lago d'Iseo
Gardone Val Trompia
10 km
5 mi
Sarnico
Iseo
A 4
Verdello
Concesio
Palazzolo sull'Oglio
A 4
43 Brescia
A21

My Day with a Bubbly Companion

The bubbles and taste of the straw-coloured Franciacorta Extra Brut are just like champagne. Just don't call it 'prosecco' – that would be an insult to the winemakers here. And, since the best sparkling wine in Italy is that from Franciacorta, it is often referred to 'Italian champagne'. Let's test the quality ourselves...

9am: From the Motorway...

To make the most of the day, we leave Desenzano del Garda for the motorway, heading in the direction of Milan, and exit at Rovato. Decide in advance who is going to do the driving and who can drink. In Italy the drink-driving limit is 0.5 milligrams of alcohol per millilitre of blood (UK: 0.8). Non-compliance can lead to draconic fines. A traditional wine-tasting, however, does not actually involve drinking, but tasting, spitting it out again. This also applies to Franciacorta: sip a little of the (sparkling) wine, let it unfold its aroma, 'swirl' it in your mouth, don't actually drink it but spit it out instead.

9.30am: ...to the Vineyards

Franciacorta (www.franciacorta.com) is not only a wine-growing area but covers some 50km² (19mi²) and comprises 23 *comune*. It is a beautiful spot to the south of ⑩ ★★ Lago d'Iseo with the charm of an age long

9:30am: ...to the Vineyards

past. The little village shops, the *alimentari*, smell of a mixture of salami and cleaning liquids, the shelves are jam-packed, *mortadella* is cut in huge slices and the proprietor himself wraps everything up carefully in brown paper bags.

10am: 'Beautiful View' Tours

The tour of the winery begins (book in advance under www.bellavistawine.it). "Three degrees", says Alberto Chioni from the Bellavista winery in Erbusco in a serious tone, "the annual temperature

Above left/right: the scent and taste of Franciacorta's sparkling white wines.
Opposite page: A detour to Lake Iseo leads to the magical Monte Isola.

difference between Lake Iseo and Lake Garda is exactly three degrees." The lower temperature and a few minerals more result in the essential difference between the simple Bardolino from Lake Garda and the superior wines from Franciacorta, the oenologist explains: "Whereas Lake Garda opens up to the south to the plain of the River Po, the Franciacorta hills form a barrier to the south of Lake Iseo which makes it more difficult for air that is too warm reaching the grapes." The winery with the delightful name is among the most renowned in this relatively young wine-growing district – 'Franciacorta' is an official term, recognised by the EU, used exclusively for wine produced in this area.

Noon: The Crowning Glory

Time passes quickly: the guided tour, tasting, shopping. The car boot is already half full – we've also bought a few bottles of Bellavista's full-bodied red wine. But we have to leave some room for the Franciacorta from Ca' del Bosco, also in Erbusco (www.cadelbosco.com), that is considered the very best in the region. There's no topping that, either in quality or price. The Franciacorta wine route extends for some 80km (50mi) and the vineyards cover around 2000ha (7.5mi^2); one wine-growing estate borders the

next and virtually all of them offer wine-tasting sessions – whether for reds, whites or particularly good sparkling wines. There's something here for everyone...

1pm: At the 'Four Roses'

Spaghetti can be found in Franciacorta, too, of course. However, polenta plays a more prominent role in this region. "We eat polenta with milk, cheese, salami... well, with everything really", says Signora Rosa from the *osteria* Quattro Rose in nearby Rovato. One of the 'four roses' – the proprietor's daughters – tells us what is on the menu today – and the meal is delicious!

2.30pm: A Detour to the Lake

We want to see the ❿ ★★ Lago d'Iseo as well, of course, since we're in the area. We could visit another winery or two instead, but Monte Isola has priority. It is the largest island in a lake in southern Europe, is car-free and studded with lemon trees.

6pm: Return to Desenzano

On returning to Lake Garda we freshen up and decide on whether to go to another wine-growing area nearby for an evening meal – to Valtènesi, for example, on the western side of the lake. We could try a really full-bodied red wine there – Gropello. It might not be bubbly – but we've had our share of excitement for one day!

9 ★★Bergamo

Why	The city is a UNESCO World Heritage site
Don't Miss	Take the funicular up to the Città Alta at all costs
When	Between 07:39 and 24:12 – when the funicular runs
Time	You'll need a whole day to explore the whole city
Tip	Sample the *stracciatella* – it was invented here

The Città Alta, protected by its walls and bastions, perches like an eyrie above Bergamo's modern Città Bassa. Bustling activity down below; churches, *palazzi* and *piazze* from days of old up high.

Opposite page: The interior of the cathedral in Bergamo is a joy for lovers of Baroque architecture

These two contrasting worlds are conveniently linked by a funicular: It is 240m (787ft) long and climbs 82m (269ft). The left track is 6m (20ft) shorter than the right because of the curve. On 20 September 1887, when the funicular was officially opened, the first carriage was filled with local dignitaries eager to take their place in history. Sadly, a wheel on the carriage jammed and the illustrious group had to walk back down the track.

Città Bassa

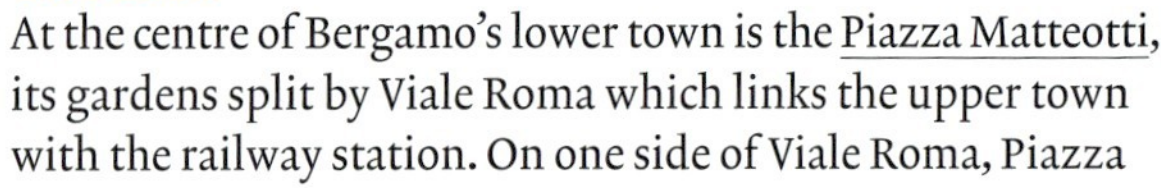

At the centre of Bergamo's lower town is the Piazza Matteotti, its gardens split by Viale Roma which links the upper town with the railway station. On one side of Viale Roma, Piazza Matteotti leads to Via XX Septembre, the city's main shopping street. On the other side stands the Teatro Donizetti. Built in the 18th century to accommodate 1300 people, the theatre was given a new façade and a new name to celebrate the 100th anniversary of the birth of Bergamo's most famous son, the composer Gaetano Donizetti (1797–1848). Beyond the theatre is the Piazza Cavour where Donizetti is depicted listening thoughtfully to the muse of song as she plays her lyre.

Bottom: The Neoclassicist façade was added in 1886

Opposite the theatre is the Sentierone, the 'Big Path' which, with its cafés and shops,

is a favourite among the local residents. The Sentierone forms part of Via Torquato Tasso. If you like religious art, follow this away from the city centre to see works by the Venetian Lorenzo Lotto (c. 1480–1556). The altarpiece of the Madonna in the church of San Bartolomeo (to the left) is one of his masterpieces.

On the Piazza G. Carrara 82, the Accademia Carrara – housed in a Late Classical building from 1796 – exhibits exceptional works by artists from Italian and international schools from the 15th to the 18th centuries. Among the highlights are portraits by *Giuliano de'Medici* (Botticelli) and *Lionello d'Este* (Pisanello) as well as the *Holy Family and St Catherine of Siena* by Lorenzo Lotto. The adjoining Galleria d'Arte Moderna e Contemporanea (Via San Tomaso 53) is devoted to contemporary art.

Città Alta

To access the pedestrianised upper town, follow Viale Roma which becomes Via Vittorio Emanuele I to the lower station of the funicular railway. In one sense this is a short ride, but in another it is the opposite. You climb on board and a few minutes later you have gone back 500 years in time, to a city of Renaissance Italy where all but essential vehicles are excluded.

From the funicular's top station cross the small square and take the narrow, winding Via Gombito uphill, passing the square and the austere 12th-century Torre Gombito to reach the Piazza Vecchia, one of the most enchanting squares in northern Italy. To your right as you enter is the Palazzo Nuovo, designed by the celebrated Renaissance architect Vincenzo Scamozzi (1552–1616) and modelled on the Sansovino library in Venice. It also houses an important library.

To the left, at the centre of the square, is the Contarini Fountain, presented to the town by Alvese Contarini, its Venetian *podestá* (governor), in 1780. Its lions, symbols of the Venetian Republic, politely hold chains in their mouths. Only 16 years later the

The *funicolare* in Bergamo links the upper town with the lower town below.

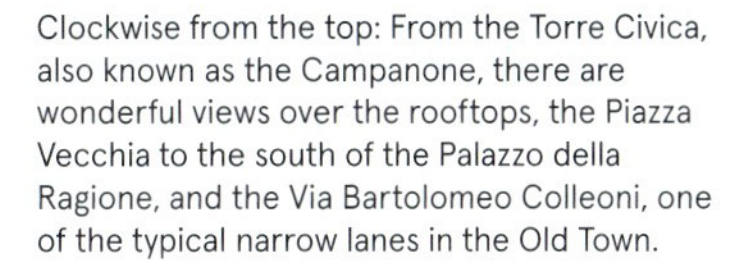

Clockwise from the top: From the Torre Civica, also known as the Campanone, there are wonderful views over the rooftops, the Piazza Vecchia to the south of the Palazzo della Ragione, and the Via Bartolomeo Colleoni, one of the typical narrow lanes in the Old Town.

inhabitants of Bergamo decided the chains of Venice were too much to bear and they tore the Venetian lion from the façade of the Torre Civica.

The Palazzo della Ragione (also known as the Palazzo Vecchio) dominates the opposite side of the square from the Palazzo Nuovo. It was rebuilt in the 16th century after a fire. The statue beside its central portico is of the poet Torquato Tasso (1544–95), about whom Goethe wrote a play and whose father came from Bergamo. Beside the *palazzo* is the Torre Civica, the old city's *campanile*, begun in the 11th century but not completed for 400 years.

Go through the arcades of the Palazzo della Ragione to reach the Piazza del Duomo, the oldest part of Bergamo. To the left is the cathedral of Sant'Alessandro with a neo-Classical façade and an impressive dome. Inside, there are several fine works of art, including *The Martyrdom of St John* by Tiepolo and bronze angels by Antonio Fontana.

Despite being the city's cathedral, the *duomo* is outshone by the church of Santa Maria Maggiore, beside it. Built in the 12th century by a city exhausted by war, plague and drought, and in need of spiritual assistance, it is plain on the outside but vast and sumptuous inside. The Cappella Colleoni with its richly decorated Renaissance façade of black, white and red marble adjoins the north porch. In 1472 Bartolomeo Colleoni, a mercenary who fought for Milan, Naples and Venice, commissioned Giovanni Antonio Amadeo to build a family mausoleum and chapel. Amadeo also created the tombs of the Colleoni family inside. The cupola frescos by Tiepolo (1789) are also noteworthy as is the *Holy Family* by the Swiss painter Angelika Kaufmann (1789).

The old streets off the Piazza del Duomo are best explored at random. Music lovers may want to see the birthplace of Gaetano Donizetti at 14 Via Borgo Canale or the museum dedicated to the composer at 9 Via Arena that includes personal objects and furnishings. Nature lovers can head for the Museo de Scienze Naturali e Caffi (Natural History Museum), housed in the 14th-century Visconti Cittadella along with the Museo Civico Archeologico (Archaeology Museum).

The Crespi d'Adda settlement is divided by a straight road. On the one side is the mill and, on the other side, roads lead off to the residential area with uniformly designed houses for the workers.

A model estate in the Province of Bergamo

Crespi d'Adda – an historical model company town in Capriate San Gervasio in the province of Bergamo – is an early example of the social commitment of enlightened industrialists. It was built from 1878 by the textile manufacturer Cristoforo Crespi and his son, Silvio, on a landscaped site not far from the River Adda which provided the mills and settlement with sufficient water. In the 1920s, more than 3000 workers were still employed here. The workers' estate – now a UNESCO World Heritage site – includes a school, an infirmary, a wash house and a church. It is still inhabited and has largely retained its original character.

INSIDER TIP The famous *stracciatella* ice cream was first created in Bergamo. The original thing is served in the **Gelateria Marianna** (Via Colle Aperto 4) in the upper town, near the funicular.

---

184 A3

Torre Civica
Piazza Vecchia ☎ 035 24 71 16
April–Oct Tue–Fri 9:30–6, Sat, Sun 9:30–8; Nov–March Tue–Fri 9:30–1, 2:30–6, Sat, Sun 9:30–86 €5

Capella Colleoni
Piazza Duomo ☎ 035 21 00 61
March–Oct Tue–Sun 9–12:30, 2–6:30; Nov–Feb Tue–Sun 9–12:30, 2–4:30
Free

Donizetti's Birthplace
Via Borgo Canale 14
☎ 035 5 29 67 11
www.donizetti.org
Sat, Sun 10–1, 3–6 Free

Museo Donizettiano
Via Arena 9 ☎ 035 24 71 16 www.bergamoestoria.it Tue–Fri 10–1, Sat, Sun 10–1, 3–6 €5

Museo di Scienze Naturali 'Enrico Caffi'
Piazza Cittadella 10 ☎ 035 28 60 11
www.museoscienzebergamo.it
April–Sep Tue–Fri 9–12:30, 2:30–6, Sat, Sun 10–13, 2:30–6:30; Oct–March 9–12:30, 2:30–5:30, Sat, Sun 10–12.30, 2:30–5:30 Uhr
€3

Museo Civico Archeologico
Piazza Cittadella 10
☎ 035 28 60 70
www.museoarcheologicobergamo.it
April–Sep Tue–Fri 9–12:30, 2:30–6, Sat, Sun 10–1, 2:30–6:30; Oct–March Tue–Fri 9–12:30, 2:30–5:30, Sat, Sun 10–12:30, 2:30–5:30 €3

Accademia Carrara
Piazza Carrara 82a
☎ 035 23 43 77 www.lacarrara.it
Wed–Mon 9:30–5:30, Fri 9:30–midnight €12

Galleria d'Arte Moderna e Contemporanea
Via San Tomaso 53
☎ 035 27 02 72 www.gamec.it
Daily 10–7, Thu until 10
€12

⑩ ★★Lago d'Iseo

Why	One of the most beautiful lakes in northern Italy
Don't Miss	See and experience
When	Grape-picking time in Franciacorta
Tip	A trip to Monte Isola is a must
Time	Around two days to avoid any rush

The 20.4km (12.7mi) long and only up to 4.1km (2.5mi) wide Lake Iseo is surrounded by the high mountain ranges of the Bergamasque Alps. Its characteristically steep banks mean that swimming is only possible at a few spots but the landscape is extremely attractive.

Opposite page: Twilight on the eastern side of the lake looking towards Peschiera Maraglio on the island Monte Isola-

You should plan enough time for a trip around Lago d'Iseo – or Sebino as it is also called – to take in its very varied scenery, to be able to enjoy leisurely strolls around the little villages and a quick visit to idyllic, car-free Monte Isola. Breathtaking views can be had from the steep west side of the lake and its craggy cliffs. On the eastern shore there are small fishing harbours, Romanesque churches and promenades lined with oleaders and palm trees.

The main town, Iseo, on the southern shore, has a beautiful medieval centre with inviting squares and twisty lanes that wind their way up the slope, as well as some good shops. Castello Oldofredi (11th century), now home to a cultural centre, lies above the Old Town. From here you get a view of the roofs of the houses and *palazzi* as well as of the several noteworthy churches from the 11th to the 17th centuries. Ferries depart from the harbour to all the larger settlements on the lake.

To the southwest of Iseo, stretching as far as Clusane, is the Torbiere del Sebino nature reserve – a peat bog with rare plants, birds and fish. Slightly above Torbiere is the convent San Pietro in Lamosa, founded in the 11th century by Cluniac monks, with frescos from the 16th century. Clusane, right on the shore of the lake, is a quiet fishing village with a large castle (14th century) with a lovely Renaissance loggia. Clusane is well known for its good fish restaurants.

Near Iseo is Sarnico, to the west of Clusane, the largest tourist resort on the lake with good watersports facilities. Good fish restaurants can be found here as well. The Art Deco villas in the Old Town and the surrounding area are especially attractive.

The jetty in Lovere on the northwestern bank: most places on the lake can easily be reached by boat.

In the extreme northwest of the lake, lively Lovere climbs up the slope from the lakeside. There is a long promenade offering lovely views over the water to the snow-capped mountains in the far distance and a medieval town centre with pretty alleyways and old towers. The Galleria dell'Accademia Tadini boasts paintings from the 14th century to the present day, sculptures, Flemish wall-hangings, porcelain and archaeological finds. A few miles east of Lovere it is well worth stopping in Pisogne to look at the church of Santa Maria della Neve (15th century) which has an impressive cycle of frescos by Girolamo Romanino from the 16th century.

Monte Isola

An excursion to the virtually traffic-free fishermen's island of Monte Isola is an unforgettable experience (see 'Magical Moment,' right). It rises some 450m (1476ft) above the water and covers a good 9km² (3.5mi²). As such, Monte Isola is the largest lake island in southern Europe and has a population of about 1700 who live in the little villages. The main centre on the island is the particularly idyllic village Peschiera Maraglio set against a green backdrop of olive, cherry and chestnut trees.

185 D3

Galleria dell'Accademia Tadini
Palazzo dell'Accademia,
Via Tadini 40 (Lungolago), Lovere
035 96 27 80

www.accademiatadini.it
May–Sep Tue–Sat 3–7, Sun 10–noon, 3–7; Oct–April Sat 3–7, Sun 10–noon, 3–7 €7

Adventures in Toyland

A miniature, mountainous island surrounded by a deep blue lake, replete with a fortress, ancient churches and houses huddled around the slopes rising above the water. From a distance you could think it were a film set with a little toy town. Monte Isola is a slice of paradise, especially with regard to its lush vegetation. Everything looks as if it has come straight out of a children's book: twisty paths link the eleven villages and hamlets with one another and call out to be explored. The pilgrimage church Madonna della Ceriola lies at the very top of the island. It is here at the very latest that you are guaranteed to get that 'magical moment' feel.

㊸ Brescia

Why	Another UNESCO World Heritage site to marvel at, just an hour or so from the lake
When	It's quieter at weekends
Don't Miss	Sight-seeing and shopping
Time	One day is probably long enough
Tip	Perhaps make a brief detour to Lonato on the way

With a population of around 195,000, Brescia is Lombardy's second largest city after Milan. The historic centre with lots of cultural sites is spanning almost 2000 years of history.

Brescia was the important centre, Colonia Civica Augusta, in Roman days. The Roman Capitolium, however, was largely buried under buildings erected in the following centuries. The Capitoline Temple (1st century), with several mosaics and a Corinthian portico, and the adjoining theatre have been excavated and partly reconstructed. Visitors to the excavation site under the Palazzo Martinengo opposite will discover a fascinating cross-section of the settlement's history spanning some 3000 years.

The Tempio Capitolino, built in 78AD, is on the narrow northern side of the Ancient Roman forum

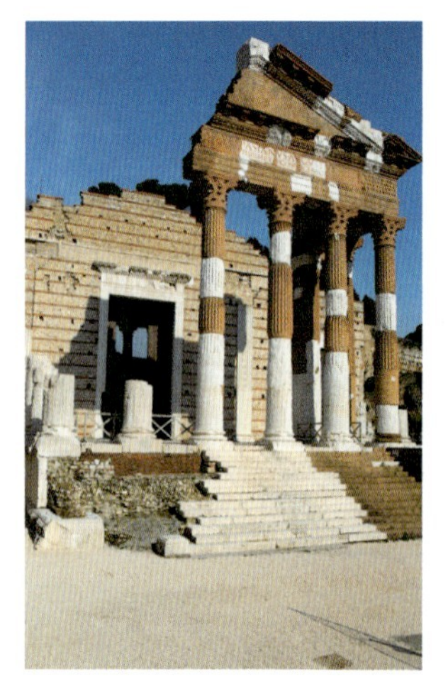

The 'long beards': Longobards in Lombardy

During the Migration Period, the Lombards or Longobards – a Germanic tribe from the north – pushed south into the region in Italy that still bears their name. According to legend, 'Longobard' derives from the 'long beards' that they tied around the chins of their womenfolk so that they looked like men and could enter a battlefield. However, it is more probable that the name comes from a long-handled axe, similar to a halberd. Seven 'Places of Power' where the Lombards erected important buildings have been combined to form

The cloister of Santa Giulia church within the convent complex – a UNESCO World Heritage site

one UNESCO World Heritage site. In 753, Desiderius, the last king of the Lombards, founded the Benedictine convent San-Salvatore-Santa-Giulia on the site of a Roman villa. The present complex incorporates the medieval church of San Salvatore, the Roman house of worship Santa Maria in Solario, Santa Giulia from the 16th century and the cloister also from this period. The exhibits tracing the long history of the city are presented in a contemporary and fitting way in this impressive setting.

Under the sign of ecclesiastical and secular power

From the 15th century onwards Brescia enjoyed an economic boom under Venetian rule. The representative buildings on the Piazza della Loggia testify to this – first and foremost the loggia itself, begun in 1492 and completed in the

The Piazza della Loggia (top) with its arcades quite clearly modelled on Venetian architecture. The New Cathedral (above), on the eastern side of the square, is named after Pope Paul VI (1963–78). The real jewel, however, is the Old Cathedral, also known as the 'Rotonda' (left)

16th century by the Venetian architects Jacopo Sansovino and Andrea Palladio. Its roof, however, was lost in a fire and a somewhat clumsy replacement added in 1914. On the south side of the *piazza* are the Monte di Pietà, the former municipal pawn office (15th century) and its more modern counterpart, Monte Nuovo. The twin-arched Renaissance building in between has a row of delicate window openings above. The three-arched loggia opposite supports the

Torre dell'Orologio, crowned by two figures which strike the clock's bell. A weekly market is held every Saturday on the Piazza della Loggia. The Viscontis built a fortress in the 15th century on the hill, Cidneo, named after a mythical Ligurian god. It now houses an arms museum as well as the Museo del Risorgimento, documenting the fight for independence. The medieval market district was pulled down in the 1920s and '30s to make way for the monumental Piazza della Vittoria. The architect was Marcello Piacentini, a precursor of the *razionalismo* style. Il Duce himself inaugurated the *piazza* in 1932.

Worldly and ecclesiastic powers rub shoulders on the rectangular Piazza Paolo VI. The Broletto, the town hall, combines architectural elements from the 12th to the 18th centuries. The Duomo Nuovo next door has a richly subdivided Baroque and Classicist façade as well as the highest dome in Italy.

The brick façade of the Duomo Vecchio by comparison is totally inconspicuous. Built in the 12th century, it comprises two cylindrical sections. Inside, steps lead down to the level of the previous building on the site, an Early Christian basilica with fragments of a mosaic preserved behind glass. The exquisite treasury – the Tesoro delle Sante Croci, that includes two reliquary crosses (14th/15th centuries) – is housed in a side chapel.

INSIDER TIP **Coffea di Nevola Ivan**, at Corso Zanardelli 26, serves excellent coffee and hot chocolate. For something more substantial try **Raffa** at no. 15 in Corso Magenta nearby.

185 D1/E2

Capitolium
Via Musei 55 030 2 07 22 56
www.bresciamusei.com
June–Sep Tue–Sun 10:30–7, Thu until 10; Oct–May Tue–Sun 9–6, Thu until 10 €8

Museo di Santa Giulia
Via Musei 81b 030 2 40 06 40
www.bresciamusei.com June–Sep Tue–Sun 10:30–7, Thu until 10; Oct–May Tue–Sun 9–6, Thu until 10
€10

Museo del Risorgimento
Via Castello 9 030 2 97 78
www.bresciamusei.com
June–Sep Tue–Sun 10:30–7, Thu until 10, Oct–May Tue–Sun 9–6, Thu until 10 €5

At Your Leisure

44 Boario Terme

Boario is named after the natural hot water that is now piped to the Thermal Establishment, a fine building set among gardens and parkland against a backdrop of high mountains. The spa owes its fame to the alchemist Paracelsus (1493–1541) who praised the healing power of the water. Close to Boario, in the Parco delle Luine, some of the rock drawings for which the Val Camonica is renowned can be seen. Alternatively, follow the road into the Val di Scalve, going through Angolo Terme, a small spa village. From here a narrow road reaches the deep-blue Lago Moro.

185 D4
Parco delle Luine
0364 54 11 00
Tue–Sun 9–noon, 2–5 Free

45 Breno

From Boario Terme the road through the Val Camonica heads towards Breno, but a short detour leads to Ésine, where the 14th-century church of Santa Maria Assunta is a National Monument, famous for its *campanile* and 15th-century frescoes. A 14th-century castle on a rocky outcrop towers over Breno.

185 E5
Castello di Breno
0364 2 29 70
Daily 10–10 Free

Idyllic countryside: the Val Camonica (here with a view of Breno Castle)

Marvels from the past: prehistoric rock engravings in the Parco Nazionale delle Incisioni Rupestri

46 Capo di Ponte

The Camuni, an ancient alpine people who created the rock engravings in Val Camonica that is now a UNESCO World Heritage site, settled in the valley in the Middle Paleolithic period and left a huge number of symbols and images. Today, the valley represents the most extensive area of prehistoric petroglyphs anywhere. The oldest of the more than 200,000 individual rock engravings have been dated to around 6000BC. There are all sorts of differnt motifs; a large number of pictures are of the animals they hunted, especially stags. Images of armed riders are equally predominant. Many of the images are difficult for us to interpret today. At Capo di Ponte, about 12km (7mi) north of Breno, there is a museum on the rock engravings together with a study centre. The Parco Nazionale delle Incisioni Rupestri has been created to help protect the images. Five easy trails lead visitors to the most attractive rocks with information boards. To see everything, allow four hours. The nearby Museo Didatico d'Arte e Vita Preistorico has a reconstructed Camuni village.

179 F5

Centro Camuno di Studi Preistorico
Via Marconi 7, Capo di Ponte
0364 4 20 91
Mon–Fri 10:30–8:30 Free

Parco Nazionale delle Incisioni Rupestri
Park next to the Chiesa Delle Sante in the village and follow the way-marked path into the park
0364 4 21 40 Tue–Sun 8:30–7
€6

Museo Didatico d'Arte e Vita Preistorico
Via Pieve San Siro 4, Capo di Ponte 0364 4 21 48
Tue–Fri 9–4, Sat, Sun, 10–5
Free

Where to... Stay

Expect to pay per double room, per night
€ under €80
€€ €80–€150
€€€ over €150

For a good night's sleep: L'Albereta in Erbusco

BERGAMO

Cappello d'Oro €€€
A Best Western 4-star hotel at the heart of the lower town. The rooms are relatively small but well decorated and furnished. Sauna, private (fee-paying) car park and an excellent restaurant. Anyone who books via the hotel website gets breakfast for 1 euro.
184 A3 Viale Papa Giovanni XXI
035 4 22 27
www.bwhotelcappellodoro-bg.it

Excelsior San Marco €€€
Midway between the funicular to the upper town and the centre of the lower town. Spacious rooms, some with a view of the upper town. Excellent restaurant.
184 A3 Piazza della Repubblica 6
035 36 61 11 www.hotelsanmarco.com

BOARIO TERME

Rizzi Aquacharme €€
One of the best hotels in the area with its own spa facilities and pool. Spacious, sprucely-kept rooms, lovely gardens, restaurant.
185 D4 Via Carducci 11 0364 53 16 17
www.rizziaquacharme.it

BRENO

Giardino €
A medium-size hotel with good facilities, ideally situated for exploring Val Camonica. Drinks in minibar €1–€1.50 each.
185 E5 Via 28 Aprile 0364 32 11 84
www.hotelgiardinobreno.com

BRESCIA

Albergo Orologio €€
This 3-star boutique hotel is just behind the Piazza Loggia. Ask for a room with a view. Care has been taken to blend antique furniture with modern amenities. Very friendly and helpful staff.
185 D1/E2 Via Beccaria 17
030 3 75 54 11
www.albergoorologio.it

ERBUSCO

L'Albereta €€€
Wonderful 5-star hotel set among the vineyards of Franciacorta. If you stay in the Cabriolet Suite you can slide back the ceiling at the press of a button and sleep under the stars...
184 C4 Via Vittorio Emanuele 23
030 7 76 05 50 www.albereta.it

Where to... Eat and Drink

Expect to pay for a three-course meal for one, excluding drinks and service
€ under €30
€€ €30–€50
€€€ over €50

BERGAMO

Borgo San Lorenzo €
Lively, colourful *osteria* packed with locals enjoying good home cooking. Pizzas are baked in a wood-burning oven and a more extensive menu for €25 is offered in the evening.
184 A3 Via San Lazzaro 8
035 24 24 52 Closed Sun

La Bruschetta €€
A beautiful building with vaulted stone ceilings. Fish and meat dishes and an excellent range of pizzas.
184 A3 Via G d'Alzano 1
035 24 89 93 Closed Mon. Dinner only

Colleoni & Dell'Angelo €€€
Housed in a medieval *palazzo* with vaulted ceilings and frescoed walls. The Bergamesque ravioli with butter and sage is hard to beat. The 5-course set menu priced at €55 is highly recommendable.
184 A3 Piazza Vecchia 7
035 23 25 96 Closed Mon and for two weeks in Aug

Da Ornella €€
Lovely little place in the Old Town specialising in polenta served with meat in cast-iron bowls. Also *polenta taragna* (cooked with butter and cheese) and rabbit.
184 A3 Via Gombito 15
035 23 27 36
Closed Thu and Fri lunch

BOARIO TERME

Airone €
The *pizzocheri* – a speciality from the Lombard region made of buckwheat and wheat flour – and polenta, and a beef stew with mushrooms and cream, are highlights on the menu in this charming restaurant.
185 D4 Via Nazionale 15
0364 53 12 76 Sat, Sun dinner only

BRESCIA

Al Teatro €
Excellent pizzeria close to the city centre. The Pizzaiolo really does make the *Diavola* devilishly hot...
185 D1/E2 Via Mazzini 36
030 4 42 51

Castello Malvezzi €€
Elegant building with a palatial atmosphere. Traditional dishes with a twist – pricey but delicious!
185 D1/E2 Via Colle San Giuseppe
030 2 00 42 24

La Sosta €€
A marvellous restaurant in the stables of the Palazzo Martinengo. Brescian specialities such as goat are on the menu. Booking in advance is advised.
185 D1/E2 Via San Martino della Battaglia 20 030 29 56 03
Closed Mon, Sun

ROVATO

Osteria Quattro Rose €€
You sit under vaulted ceilings and next to shelves stocked with wine. This is a wine cellar where food is also served by the four ladies of the house (the *quattro rose*...). The *osteria* is, after all, right in the middle of Franciacorta: the wine list, for example, lists 400 different varieties!
184 C4 Via Castello 27b 8 030 72 30 27
http://quattrorose.it Closed Thu

Where to... Shop

As major cities, both Brescia and Bergamo have large shopping areas and some out-of-town centres. Many international brands have outlets in the two towns but there are also lots of individual shops too.

BERGAMO CITTÀ BASSA

There are many boutiques for ladies' fashions in Via XX Septembre. **La Perla** (Sentierone 40) has high-quality swimwear and underclothes. For shoes look for **Pompeo** (Via XX Septembre 27), **Bruschi** (Via XX Septembre 39), **Fratelli Rossetti** (Via XX Septembre 52) and **Dev** (Via XX Septembre 85–87).
For handbags and other leather goods there is **Diana** (Via XX Septembre 40).
The area around the **Accademia Carrara** is popular with artists and there are several studios, most notably that of **Sergio Garau** (Via San Tomaso 88a), who paints on old wood and cloth. Close to Sergio's studio there is a good antique shop – **GLA Antichità** (Via Sant' Orsola 17).
The biggest department store in the city centre is **Coin** (Largo Medaglie d'Oro, Via Zambonate 11).

BERGAMO CITTÀ ALTA

The upper town is both much smaller and much more given over to outlets for visitors with its restaurants, bars, etc. But there are some gems, including Babilonia (Via Gombito 12d) which sells chic ladies' clothing. Opposite the restaurant Colleoni on the Piazza Vecchia is Daniela Gregis who designs and makes one-off articles and has already been featured in Vogue. For menswear Franco Loda (Via Gombito 17) is excellent, whereas Cesare Albert (Via Bartolomeo Colleoni 5b) is the place to go for some of the best children's clothes in the area. Brivio (Via B Colleoni 19a) has excellent jewellery and silverware. For gifts, the candles at RR Candele (Via B Colleoni 15m) are good value.
Cooperativa Libraria Il Quarttiere (Via Gombito 24a) is a well-stocked stationers with a good range of toys as well.

BRESCIA

For jewellery, the following are certainly worth a look: Giarin (Via San Martino della Battaglia), try Ghidini, (Corso Magenta 8b) for unusual, exciting designs and Emozioni d'Oro, (Via Valcamonica 17). For shoes try Fratelli Rossetti (Corso Zanardelli 1) and Romano (Corso Palestro 13).
Many designer fabrics can be found at Casa Sovrana in Portici X Giornate.
And for antiques look out for Cronos, Galleria al Duomo (Via X Giornate), Ceralacca (Via Fratelli Porcellana 42), Antic Oro (Vicolo della Speranza 3d), for both old and new jewellery and Rino Fossati (Via Beccaria 3a). The biggest department store in the city centre is Coin at the corner of Corso Magenta and Via San Martino della Battaglia. The huge out-of-town Franciacorta Outlet Village is on the Bergamo road, at the 'Ospitaletto' exit on the A4. There are some 160 shops of internationally well-known brands from Adidas to Timberland, providing a massive selection at low prices. And if you fancy a break while shopping, there are around a dozen bars and restaurants to quench your thirst and satisfy your hunger. Open daily until 8pm (www.franciacortaoutlet.it).

Where to... Go Out

WALKING

Both Bergamo and Brescia are excellent centres from which to explore the valleys that head north towards the Alps. North of Bergamo are the Val Brembana and Val Seriana. Val Seriana is famous for the Cascata del Serio.
North of Brescia, there is lovely countryside and good walking in Val Camonica, famous for its rock engravings, Val Sabbia and Val Trompia, as well as in the Franciacorta, northwest of the city.

GOLF

There are several golf courses in the area close to Bergamo and Brescia. Francaciorta Golf Club has an unusual 'Wine Golf Course' (www.franciacortagolfclub.com), with each of the 9 holes having names such as 'Brut', 'Saten' and 'Rosé'.

OTHER SPORTS

There are opportunities for tennis, squash, etc. in the sports centres in each of the cities. From Brescia, the watersports facilities on the western side of Lake Garda can be easily reached.

Stronghold of the muses: the Donizetti Theatre, Bergamo.

Few races are as well known as the Mille Miglia that was held from 1927 until 1957 and again from 1977 onwards – albeit it now for classic and vintage cars; an event that has always made the hearts of sports car enthusiasts beat faster.

THEATRE AND CINEMA

There are cinemas in Brescia and Bergamo. At **Manerbio** – just off the A21 *autostrada* south of Brescia – there is a multi-screen cinema.
The **Donizetti Theatre** in Bergamo has four seasons each year. The opera season is from September to December, the drama season from November to April. There is a jazz festival in February and a season of dance/ballet from January to April.
The **Teatro Grande** in Brescia has an opera season from September to November, a drama season from November to April and a season of concerts from October to March. Brescia also has two other theatres, **Teatro di Santa Chiara** and **Teatro Sancarlino**.

NIGHTLIFE

There are a few discos in the Bergamo area: **Capogiro** (Strada Statale Briantea), for instance, and **Setai** which plays house, underground and dance music (Località Portico). There are also a dozen discos and nightclubs in Brescia itself. At present the popular ones are **Pepe** (Via Orzinuovi 129) and **Planet Agency** (Via Vergnano 65).

FESTIVALS

Brescia hosts the **Festa dell' Opera** in September and a series of organ concerts from mid-September to mid-October in its churches.
Most famous of all is the **Mille Miglia** (1,000mi/ 1,600km) car race which, starting in Brescia, was held annually until 1957, when it was stopped after a series of accidents involving the deaths of spectators. In 1977 the event was revived as a three-day veteran car rally held in May, running from Brescia to Ferrara, then to Rome and back to Brescia.

MARKETS

There is an **antiques market** on the Piazza Cittadella in Bergamo's Città Alta on the third Sunday of the month. There is also a **book fair** at the Sentierone in April and May.

The towns and villages on the west side of the lake only turned into tourist honeypots after the Gardesana Occidentale was opened.

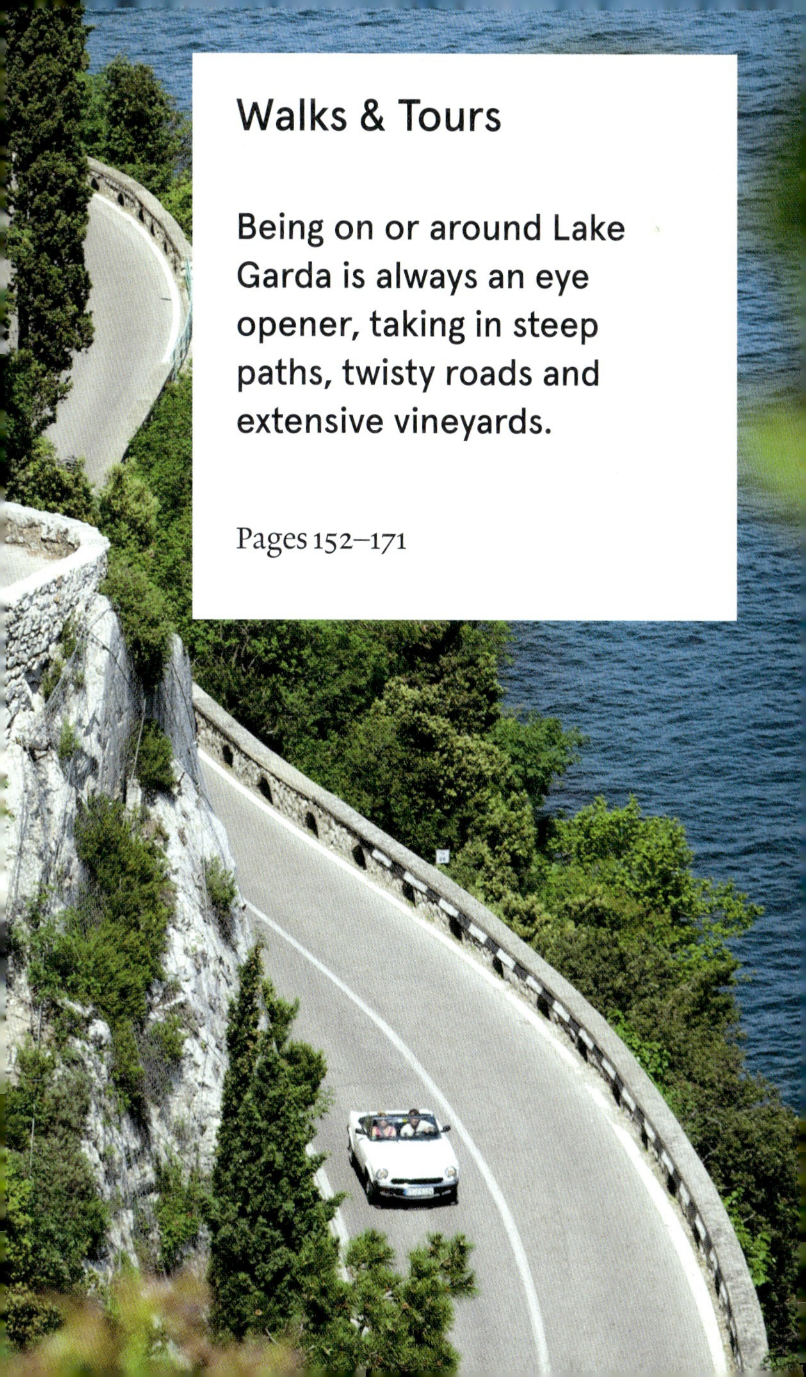

Walks & Tours

Being on or around Lake Garda is always an eye opener, taking in steep paths, twisty roads and extensive vineyards.

Pages 152–171

Monte Baldo

What	Hiking in spectacular mountain scenery
Distance	8km (5mi)
Time	2½ hours
Start/End	Lower cable-car station, Malcesine (https://funiviedelbaldo.it) 187 D4

This exhilarating walk lets you enjoy the countryside in its most natural form, taking in the hugely varying endemic flora and fauna found in the several different climatic zones, as well as providing panoramic views of the lake. Take a rain and windproof jacket even if you do set out under a cloudless sky, as the temperature on the ridge will be cooler than at the lakeside and thunderstorms can brew up quickly at the top. Stout shoes and sunglasses are needed in summer, as well as sun cream and a hat which is very necessary at this altitude.

Opposite page: The 4325m (2¾mi)-long journey with the 'Funivia Malcesine – Monte Baldo' takes less than 10 minutes. It is one of the most modern cable-cars in the world with a cabin that slowly turns a full 360 degrees on its way up to the top at 2000m (6562ft).

1–2

Take the cable-car to the summit of Monte Baldo and immerse yourself in a unique world full of both small and larger natural wonders. As the slopes of the mountain were never covered by a glacier during the Ice Age, many relict plants survived the long periods of cold including a number of endemic species.

2–3

Leave the cable-car and turn right, descending briefly (past a café) to reach an electricity sub-station and a path junction. Go straight ahead towards the ski-lift.

3–4

Keep to the right of the ski lift and follow the marked route 651 as it climbs over rough, then much gentler, terrain to a chair lift.

4–5

The end point of the shorter walk is now in sight. Go through the fence into the nature reserve and follow the clear path

MALCESINE
MONTE BALDO

'The reward lies along the way' – and this applies to Monte Baldo, too, where it is always worthwhile stopping to take in the stunning panoramic view.

along the ridge studded with dwarf-pines. The grassy terrain gradually gives way to rougher ground but the going is never very arduous and the path is always obvious. The objective of the short walk, Cima delle Pozzette, at 2132m (6972ft), is reached after about 1.5 hours' walking. On a clear day the view is breathtaking, extending west to Monte Rosa, taking in the Adamello and the Alps north of it, and east as far as the Julian Alps. Inevitably, however, the eye is drawn to Lake Garda, stretching out below the ridge.

The walk can be extended. The long walk is, therefore, 4½ hours long, much of it above 2000m (6540ft) and half of it on a very rugged mountain and should only be attempted by experienced hillwalkers. Please be very cautious and inform yourselves about weather conditions before setting out.

5–6

Route 651 continues straightforwardly from Cima delle Pozzette, dropping down almost 200m (654ft) then rising towards the summit of Cima del Longino (2179m/7096ft).

From here the path becomes more rugged and spectacular, going over Cima Val Finestra (2084m/6815ft) then edging east around the cliffs of Cima Valdritta. It now becomes a true mountain path, experience and sure-footedness being required to follow the northern ridge to the summit of Cima Valdritta (2218m/7253ft), the highest point of Monte Baldo. From Cima Valdritta, do the route in reverse, taking great care on descents, to Cima delle Pozzette and back to the cable-car top station that will take you back down to the lake.

Tremosine & Tignale

What	Twisty tour by car with breathtaking views
Distance	45km (28mi)
Time	2 hours
Start	Limone sul Garda ⤉187 D4
End	Gargnano ⤉186 C3

Above the northwestern shore of Lake Garda lie two high plateaus of alpine meadows. The road to them is twisty and occasionally tortuous but the views of the mountains to the north, mountain villages and Lake Garda are breathtaking.

Opposite page: The 'scary terrace' at Hotel Paradiso in Pieve di Tremosine (www.terrazza delbrivido.it) juts out several feet over a sheer drop

1–2

At the southern end of Limone sul Garda is a large car park used by day visitors to the town. From here, take the route back to the Gardesana Occidentale, the road that follows the western shore of the lake and turn left towards the towns on the lake to the south. Ignore the first turn on the right (signed for Tremosine) and go past a sign welcoming you to the district of Tremosine.

2–3

The Gardesana Occidentale now goes through a series of four tunnels. The first two are relatively short (about 100m), the third is longer (about 500m), the fourth about 2.5km (1.5mi). About 100m after exiting from this fourth tunnel, take the road on the right (Via Benaco) signed Tremosine.

3–4

Go through a short tunnel, beyond which the road becomes very narrow, climbing steeply uphill with winding bends and hairpins to reach a *galleria* (an open-sided tunnel). Beyond this the road widens and offers the first view of the lake to your right. Go through another tunnel, noting the arched roof: beware – if a lorry or bus is coming the other way it will be in the middle of the road. Beyond the tunnel the road becomes single track again with passing places.

4–5

This is a delightful section of road, with a stream in the wooded gorge to your right and a small bridge that diverts another stream over the road to fall as a waterfall beside it. However, the driving requires concentration and skill if you meet oncoming traffic. Patience and goodwill are required by both drivers.

Go over a tiny bridge to reach a section of road carved out of the mountain: the gorge here is very narrow. At a sign for the Hotel Paradiso a bridge appears ahead and above: you will actually cross this soon as the road doubles back on itself to gain height. Just beyond this the La Forra Ristorante is reached – a good place for an early cup of coffee. The most tortuous section of the drive is now over.

5–6

The road now widens and soon you arrive in Pieve. The route bears right here (signed Voltino), but it is worth stopping in the village to visit the Miralago restaurant, a good place for lunch. The restaurant is cantilevered over a stupendous drop above Lake Garda, so the views are amazing, as is the local cuisine. (To reach the Miralago, go into Piazza Fossato and, with the tourist office behind you, walk straight ahead.) The tourist office has information on the Parco Regionale dell'Alto Garda Bresciano, set up to protect the natural scenery of Tremosine and Tignale and the mountains to the north and west. The wildlife of the park includes roe deer, several varieties of frogs and toads, salamanders, the sulphur-yellow Cleopatra butterfly and, in the high hills, the European brown bear, which has recently returned to the area and is being monitored as part of the 'Life Ursus' project.

6–7

Back on the drive, follow the road towards Voltino, with terrific views of the mountain villages of the Tremosine. Beyond Priezzo where the church dates from the 7th century the road is slightly wider and the countryside more open. Go through a short tunnel: the road now winds up to the village of Villa. Just outside the village there is a viewpoint from which to admire the terraced village.

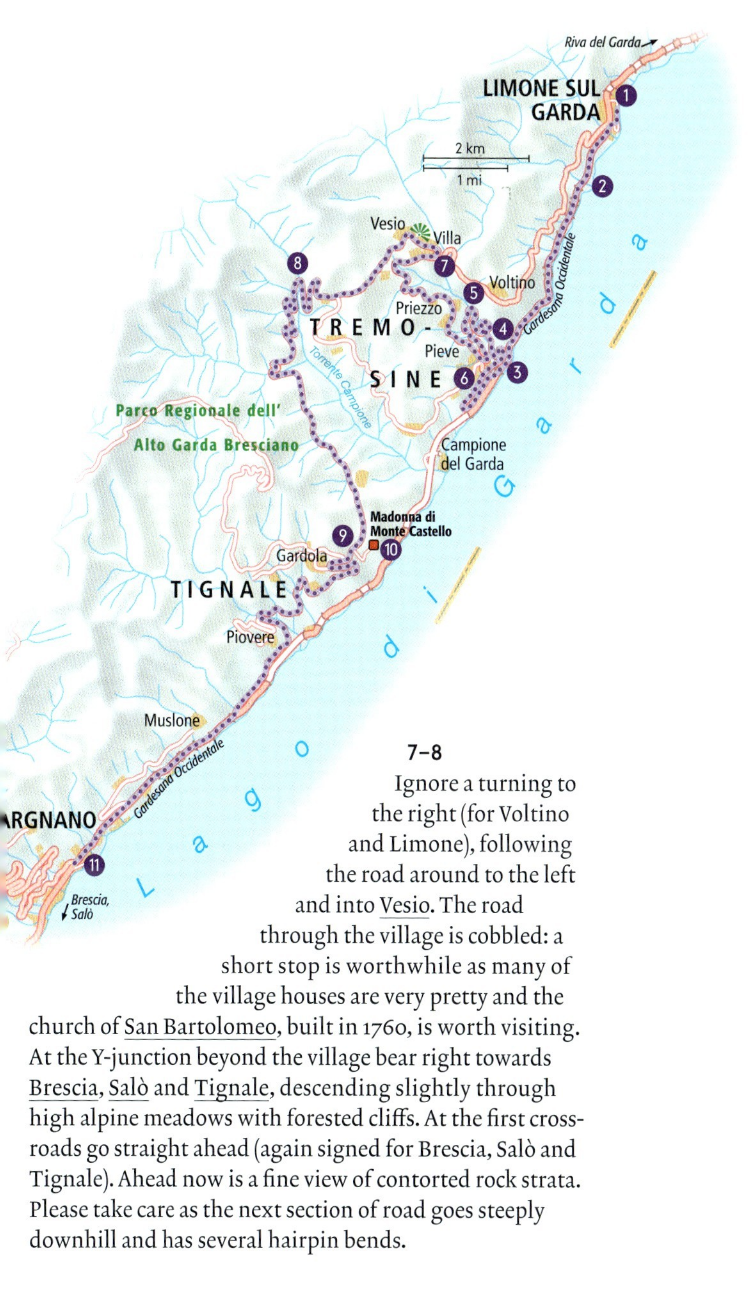

7–8

Ignore a turning to the right (for Voltino and Limone), following the road around to the left and into Vesio. The road through the village is cobbled: a short stop is worthwhile as many of the village houses are very pretty and the church of San Bartolomeo, built in 1760, is worth visiting. At the Y-junction beyond the village bear right towards Brescia, Salò and Tignale, descending slightly through high alpine meadows with forested cliffs. At the first crossroads go straight ahead (again signed for Brescia, Salò and Tignale). Ahead now is a fine view of contorted rock strata. Please take care as the next section of road goes steeply downhill and has several hairpin bends.

8–9

Cross a river (the Torrente Campione) and start to ascend, again through a series of hairpins. The road then descends and climbs to reach a sign welcoming you to Tignale. Just beyond this you will have a glimpse of Lake Garda and the road becomes a double-width carriageway for the first time. Ignore the road ahead signed for Tignale, staying with the 'main' road to reach a signed turn to the left for the Eremo di Monte Castello.

9–10

Turn left for the church and park below on the large car park on the main road. If you don't fancy the 20-min. walk, you can try driving up the single track road that becomes very steep.

A sharp hairpin is followed by an even steeper section that leads to an archway barely wide enough for a car. At the church of Madonna di Monte Castello itself there are only about 12 parking spaces.

10–11

Just follow the sun: Instead of taking the car up twisty narrow roads try a more breezy alternative and make a trip on or around the lake on a Vespa

After admiring the church and the view from it, retrace your way back to the main road, looking out for roadside shrines with frescoes of the Stations of the Cross that may have escaped your attention on the drive up, and turn left. Go through Gárdola, bearing left (signed Salò/Riva) and descending, with an expanding view of the lake: there are a couple of places on this road which offer fine views across the lake to Malcesine, with Monte Baldo rising above it.

Ignore the turning for Piovere and continue downhill to rejoin the Gardesana Occidentale. Turn right and then left to reach Gargnano, the final destination on this tour.

North of Riva

What	A round-trip between the water and overhanging cliffs
Distance	70km (43mi)
Time	2½ hours
Start/End	Porta San Michele, Riva del Garda ⟶ 187 D5

North of Riva lie the huge, spiky, rocky peaks of the Brenta Dolomites. On this drive you will be able to enjoy the craggy scenery that has made the Brenta region so famous, but still be back in time for dinner.

1–2

At Porta San Michele in Riva turn left on to Viale Dante, then right on to Viale Prati. At the stop sign turn right along Viale Giuseppe Canella. Now at the roundabout (Largo Marconi) take the second exit, signposted Varone/Tenno (Via dei Tigli). Bear right, then left, following signs for the Cascata del Varone.

View of Riva, seen from the north – spring on Lake Garda

2–3

Keep ahead along the road as it bears left, with a view ahead of magnificent rock faces and mountains and a small vineyard on your left. You now start climbing and will soon see the entrance to the Cascata del Varone on your left. There is a picnic area and café here, but it is probably too early in the drive unless you are planning to view the falls.

3–4

Continue through Gavazzo, a picturesque village of old houses with shutters and colourful window boxes, going steeply uphill. There is now an expanding view towards Riva and the lake, with occasional parking places to take full advantage of it. The road ahead climbs through several hairpin bends, with olive trees and vines to your left and right, and the occasional orange tree as well.

Alpine farmsteads are perched just below the tree line.

4–5

Go through Cologna, just beyond the village there is a viewpoint to your right: from here you can see Monte Baldo and the northern lake as well as more local views. The hillside is terraced for olive trees and vines. There is another picnic area on the right just before reaching Tenno. At Tenno the old castle is now the Ristorante Castello, an amazing place to have lunch. Beyond, the hairpin bends continue, as do the marvellous views of the mountains.

5–6

Go through Ville del Monte, a lovely mixture of architecture, the roofs having the familiar semi-circular tiles which appear to have been thrown into position. Beyond, Lago di Tenno lies below to your right. Depending upon the weather the lake appears emerald green or turquoise blue – but at all times it is extremely picturesque. After a short descent through woodland you start to ascend again. Another possible lunch spot – Pizzeria da Lalucio – is soon passed and there is a picnic site just ahead on an alpine meadow.

6–7

You now start to descend. Bear right towards Ponte Arco, ignoring the road to Fiavè, and observe the impressive views of the jagged rock faces ahead. Go through Dasindo, a very pretty village, then notice, at Vigo Lomaso, that there are 'Caution Deer' signs. It would add another dimension to the drive to see one, but they are elusive creatures. Go past the beautiful Villa Lutti, with its curious round tower, and descend steeply through several hairpin bends to reach Ponte Arco. Turn right on to the road for Trento. To the left, the Al Pont is an excellent stop for a cup of coffee or a snack.

7–8

Drive through Terme di Comano and follow the narrow, winding road past overhanging cliffs to the right with the Sarca river to the left. On the next section of road you climb

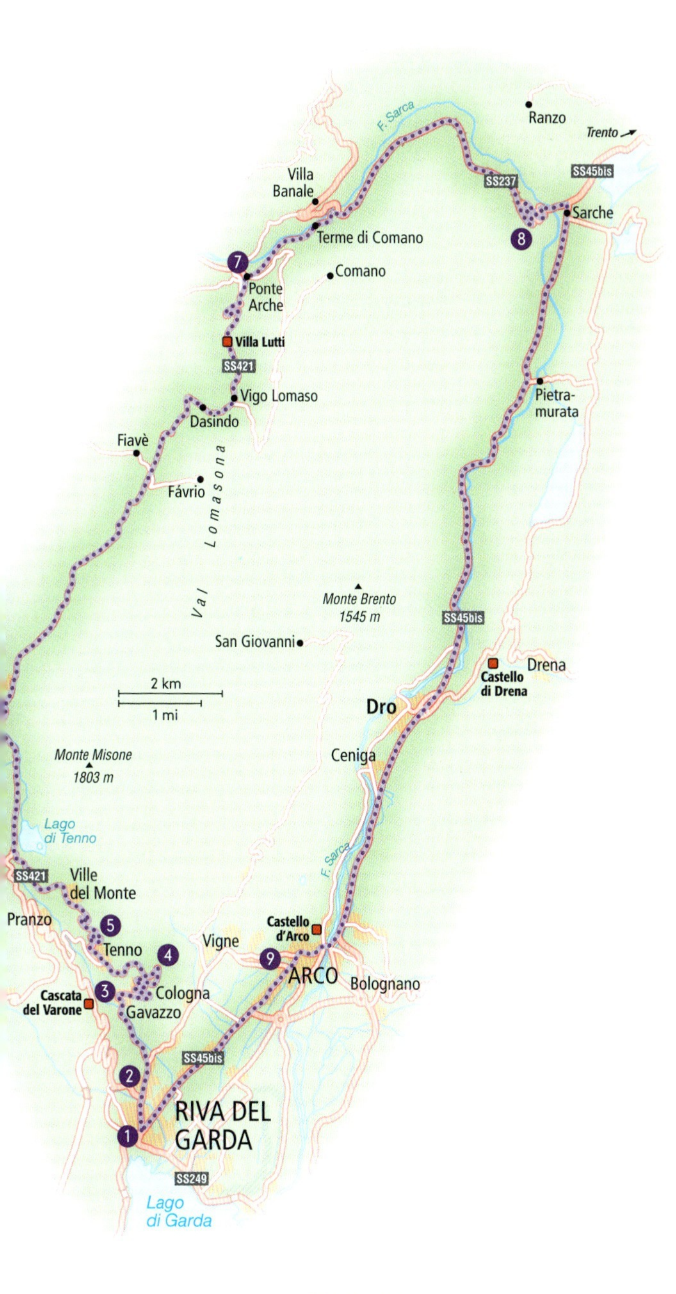

F. Sarca
Ranzo
Trento
SS45bis
Villa
Banale
SS237
Sarche
Terme di Comano
8
7
Comano
Ponte
Arche
Villa Lutti
SS421
Vigo Lomaso
Pietra-
murata
Dasindo
Fiavè
Fávrio
Val Lomasona
Monte Brento
1545 m
SS45bis
San Giovanni
Drena
Castello
di Drena
2 km
1 mi
Dro
Ceniga
Monte Misone
1803 m
Lago
di Tenno
F. Sarca
SS421
Ville
del Monte
Pranzo
5
Castello
d'Arco
Tenno
4
Vigne
9
ARCO
Bolognano
Cascata
del Varone
3
Cologna
Gavazzo
SS45bis
2
RIVA DEL
GARDA
1
SS249
Lago
di Garda

steeply with Dolomite-like rock faces and towering peaks to your left. Go through a very long tunnel, after which there is a view of the mountains and huge rock faces before plunging into another long tunnel which ends with a *galleria*. There are further tunnels: after the fourth there is a picnic area on the left below impressive cliffs. As you start to descend into Sarche there is a sign for the Zona del Vino Santo DOC with a list of *cantine* that are well-known for their sweet wines should you wish to extend the drive. Sarche is famous among geologists because of the marocche, a remarkable area of huge boulders – the result of three post-glacial landslides.

8–9

Cross the Sarca and turn right at the T-junction towards Riva del Garda. At the roundabout go straight on towards Arco/Riva, driving through a vast vineyard, left and right, which extends for about 2km (1 mile). Recross the river and look out for the Castello di Drena perched on the hillside to your left. The castle was built by the lords of Arco in the late 12th century to defend the valley. The Arco valley is one of only a handful of readily passable routes through the mountains and the Arco lords had constantly to be prepared to meet invading armies. The castle is open to the public. Ahead you can now also see the castle at Arco, perched on a pyramid of rock. Bear right, crossing the Sarca again to reach Arco. If you are stopping here, turn right after crossing the bridge for the car park.

9–1

At the traffic lights go left towards Riva. Soon you will pass a park with a fountain on your right. At the roundabout go straight ahead towards Riva, passing several garden centres. Go past a sign welcoming you to Riva even though there is still a little way to go to reach the town. Go straight ahead through two sets of traffic lights. You will soon reach the Astoria Park Hotel on your right and, to the left opposite the hotel, is the ultra-modern church of San Josep. Continue in this direction to reach the roundabout where you turned off to Varone at the start of the drive. From here it is about 1km (0.6 mile) back to Porta San Michele.

Local Vineyards

What	A trip around (and to) famous vineyards
Distance	80km (50mi)
Time	3 hours, but longer if wine outlets are visited and lunch is taken
Start/End	Bardolino 186 C2

Close to Lake Garda's southeastern tip grapes are grown that are used to make some of Italy's most famous wines, Bardolino and Valpolicella. There is a Strada del Vino through the Bardolino area, but there is no 'official' route through the Valpolicella area. This is a suggested route that links the two areas, making the most of each. The middle section of the route is passed in both directions, a necessary reversal to get between the two.

1–2

Start in Bardolino, at the tourist information office on the Gardesana Orientale. From the office, head north (towards Garda), but immediately, at the first roundabout, take the first right turn (Via Croce) which is signposted to the Wine Museum. Ignore the sign for the Strada del Vino on the right, continuing straight on and passing a sign for Affi with a fine row of trees to your right and a boatyard to your left: the first Bardolino vines are to your left after this. Continue through olive groves, soon passing Costadoro, a Bardolino vineyard and then Frantoio where local olive oil can be bought, with good views of the mountains ahead.

Whoever said that wine is only to be drunk? A massage with oil made from grape pips makes you feel good as well – as here, for example, in Bardolino.

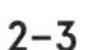

2–3

At the roundabout go straight across (on the road signposted Affi), passing the Naiano vineyard. At the next roundabout turn right, passing the La Canova winery. Soon after, bear left along a road signed for Modena/Brennero A22 and Piovezzano, passing through olive groves to reach a little lake on the right. Cross over the A22 *autostrada* and pass the Effegi and Goretex factories.

3–4

At the stop sign turn left towards Sant'Ambrogio di Valpolicella, looking out for the fascinating boulders. Now, at the T-junction turn left. Go past the Stone Gallery with its gigantic pieces of stone. The Valpolicella quarries produced the *rossa di Verona* marble from which many of the buildings in the city were constructed. Continue through the pretty village of Sega, then bear right towards the road (12) and go over the Adige River.

4–5

At the T-junction turn right and drive through Domegliara. At the crossroads take the road left signed Sant'Ambrogio and Negrar and after about 100m (go under a railway bridge and slightly uphill) turn right towards Negrar/San Pietro in Cariano. Continue uphill and go straight ahead at the traffic lights and under a bridge. Your first Valpolicella vineyard is to your right with terraced vineyards to your left. Go under another bridge.

5–6

Go straight ahead at the roundabout (signed San Pietro in Cariano/Pedemonte) and again at the traffic lights. Do not bear left with the road but keep going ahead (leaving the main road) past the Famila supermarket. The road narrows just before a stop sign: turn right at the traffic lights following the sign for Negrar. After passing shops, turn left at the traffic lights. There are beautiful views here, with Monte Baldo on your left and forested hills to your right. The Cantina Sociale Valpolicella organisation sells local wines. Go through Negrar – a pretty village with a picturesque 12th-century church and *campanile* to your left and a river to your right.

6–7

Look out for a left turn signposted Prun/Torbe. The Vecchia, on the left when heading for Torbe, is excellent for a short break or for lunch. The road beyond rises steeply through

Delicious wines maturing in the Barrique barrels at Zeni winery (above) in Bardolino (top and right)

a series of hairpins with excellent views all around. Go through the picturesque village of Torbe and continue uphill. Bear left towards Cerna/Santa Cristina, soon passing incredible marble quarries to the right.

7–8

At the stop sign, turn left for Marano di Valpolicella. Soon you pass a picnic area, with stone tables and seats. There are excellent views of woodland here and as the road is usually very quiet this could be an alternative lunch spot. Back on the road, as you descend there are spectacular views to forested mountainside. Continue downhill, passing a lake, through the village of San Rocco, then through Pezza. A series of downhill hairpin bends takes you to Marano di Valpolicella, with its vast domed church. Go through Prognol and Valgatara, passing the San Rustico and Michele Castellona wine outlets and the traffic lights at San Floriano. In the next village, San Pietro in Cariano, at no. 7, Via Cà dell' Ebreo, the winery Vantini Luigi e Figli has a wide selection. Founded in 1908, it also offers guided tours and wine tasting. After all, you can't finish the tour without sampling an Amarone – considered one of Italy's very best red wines.

8–9

Head west to Sant'Ambrogio di Valpolicella. Go straight ahead at the traffic lights (signed Domegliara), with excellent mountain views ahead. At the stop sign turn left (straight ahead is a No Through Road) and at the traffic lights turn right towards Pastrengo.

9–10

At the next traffic lights turn left towards Pastrengo, passing a huge marble works to your right and a sign which marks the end of Valpolicella. Go over a river bridge, then bear left

onto a road signed to Pastrengo/Lazise. Go uphill, then bear right towards Lazise.

10–1

Bear left at the Y-junction, heading towards Lazise. Cross the A22 *autostrada*, with you last views of Monte Baldo beyond the conifers on your right. Go past the Bardolino vineyards of Ca' Furia, Podere San Giorgio and Girasole, then turn left towards Lazise. The Azienda Agricola della Pieve – olive oil sales and an *agriturismo* site – is to your left. Go under a bridge with a little lake on your left, passing through Montiana. This section of the route passes through pleasant country and you soon have your first glimpse of Lake Garda. At the stop sign turn right to reach Lazise, following the lakeside road north from there to return to Bardolino.

Photographing in Garda with the Isola di Trimelone in the background.

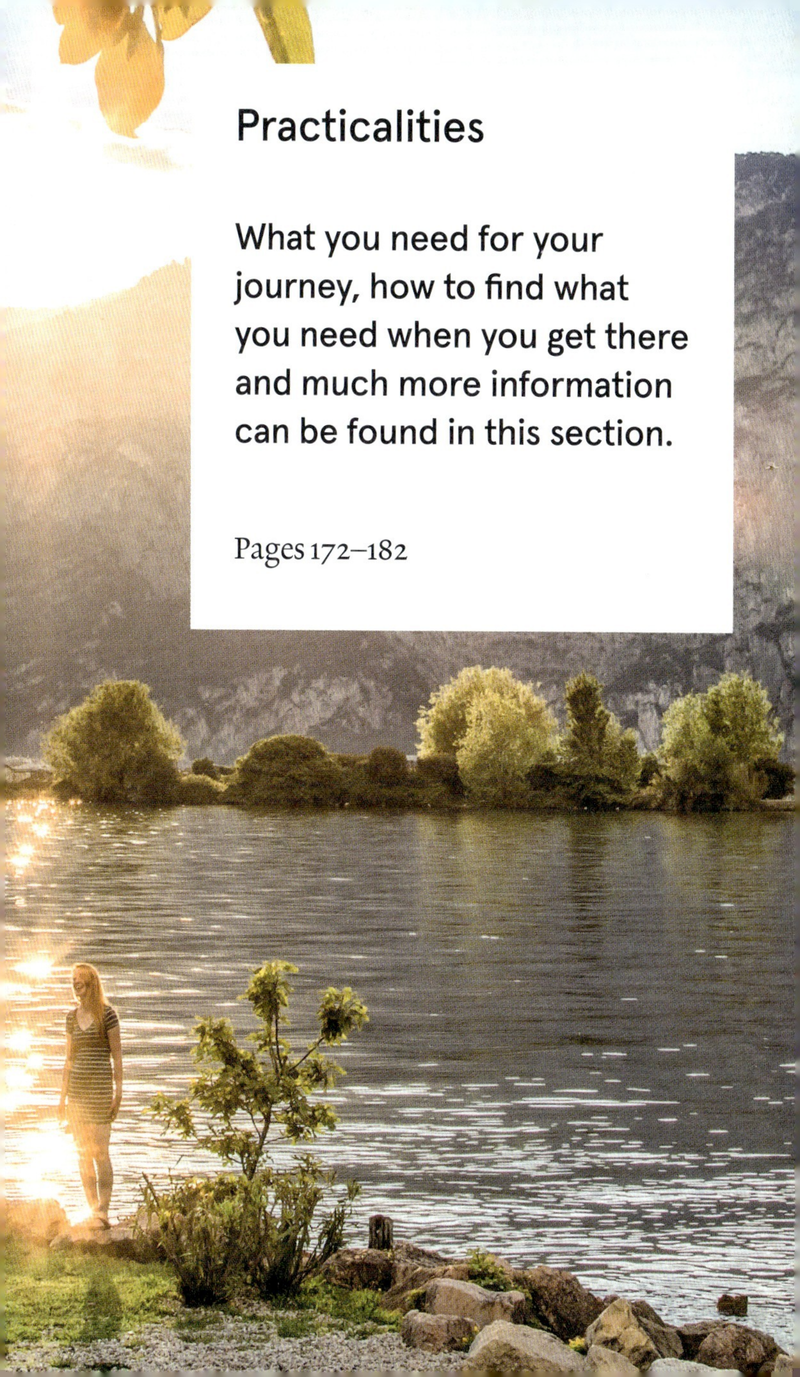

Practicalities

What you need for your journey, how to find what you need when you get there and much more information can be found in this section.

Pages 172–182

BEFORE YOU GO

Advance Information
Websites
www.visitgarda.com: For all three regions on and around the lake: Trentino, Veneto, Lombardia.
www.ristogarda.com: For all foodies: restaurants, recipes, regional specialities.

Italian State Tourist Office (ENIT, www.enit.it)
In the UK: 1 Princes Street, London W1R 8AY, tel: 020 74 08 12 54
In the US: Suite 1565, 630 Fifth Avenue, New York, NY 10111, tel: (212) 245 56 18
In Australia: Level 24, 44 Market Street, Sydney NSW 2000, tel: (02) 92 62 16 66
In Canada: Suite 907, 175 Bloor Street East, Toronto M4W 3R8, tel: (416) 925 48 82

Bergamo: Via Aeroporto 13, 24050 Bergamo-Orio al Serio, tel: 035 32 04 02, www.visitbergamo.net
Brescia: Via Luigi Einaudi 23, 25121 Brescia, tel: 030 372 54 03, www.brescia tourism.it
Lago di Garda: Most tourist information offices are in the centres of each town or village, as in Sirmione, or in the bus station as in Malcesine. The main tourist information offices on Lago di Garda, that comes under the Veneto local authority can be found under www.tourism.verona.it/en; for the Trentino area, see: www.gardatrentino.it/en and for the west side of the lake, in Lombardy, see: www.gardalombardia.com.
Lago d'Iseo and Franciacorta: Lungolago Marconi 2c, 25049 Iseo, tel: 030 374 87 33, www.visitlakeiseo.info
Trentino: Via Romagnosi 11, 38122 Trento, tel: 046 121 93 00, www.visittrentino.it
Verona: Via Degli Alpini 9 (Piazza Bra), 37121 Verona, tel: 045 806 86 80, www.veronatouristoffice.it

Concessions
Young visitors and children under 18 from EU countries are entitled to free entrance or reduced rates to most galleries. Similar concessions are available to senior citizens over 65. A passport is required as proof of age.

Currency & Foreign Exchange
Currency The currency in Italy is the euro (€). There are 1, 2, 5, 10, 20 and 50 cent coins and €1 and €2 coins. Notes are issued in denominations of €5, €10, €20, €50, €100, €200 and €500.
Exchange Most major travellers' cheques – the best way to carry money – can be changed at exchange kiosks *(cambio)* at the airports, at main railway stations and in exchange offices near major tourist sights. Many banks also have exchange desks but queues can be long.
Credit cards Most credit cards (*carta di credito* – but frequently the word tessera is used for 'card') are widely accepted in major hotels, restaurants and shops, but cash is often preferred in smaller establishments and generally everywhere in the more rural areas. Credit cards can also be used to obtain cash from ATM cash dispensers.

Customs
Within the EU, customs duty is generally not payable on goods for private use. Restrictions only apply over a certain quantity (e. g. a max. of 800 cigarettes, 10 l spirits and 90 l wine is permitted for each person over 17). For non-EU citizens, the following import allowances apply: 200 cigarettes or 100 cigarillos or 50 cigars or 250 g tobacco, 2 l wine or other drinks with an alcohol content of up to 22 % and 1 l spirits with more than 22 %.

Electricity
The current is 220 volts AC, 50 cycles. Plugs are of the round two-pin continental type; UK and North American visitors will require an adaptor. North American visitors should check whether 110/120-volt AC appliances require a voltage transformer.

Embassies
British Embassy
Via XX Settembre 80/a, 00187 Roma
Tel: +39 06 42 20 00 01, www.gov.uk/world
U.S. Embassy
Via Vittorio Veneto 121, 00187 Roma
Tel: +39 06 4 67 41, https://it.usembassy.gov
Irish Embassy
Villa Spada, Via G. Medici, 1, 00153 Roma
+39 06 5 85 23 81, www.dfa.ie/irish-embassy

Australian Embassy
Via Antonio Bosio, 5, 00161, Rome
Tel: +39 06 8 52 721
italy.embassy.gov.au/rome/home.html

Canadian Embassy
Via Salaria, 243, 00199 Roma
Tel: +39 06 85 44 41
www.canadainternational.gc.ca/italy-italie

National Holidays

1 Jan	*Capodanno* – New Year's Day
6 Jan	Epiphany
Mar/Apr	*Pasqua* – Easter
Mar/Apr	*Pasquetta* – Easter Monday
25 Apr	Liberation Day
1 May	*Festa del Lavoro* – Labour Day
24 June	*San Giovanni* – St John's Day
15 Aug	Assumption of the Virgin Mary
1 Nov	*Tutti Santi* – All Saints' Day
8 Dec	Immaculate Conception
25 Dec	*Natale* – Christmas Day
26 Dec	*Santo Stefano* – St Stephen's Day

Health

Insurance Nationals of EU countries can get medical treatment at a reduced cost in Italy with the relevant documentation (on presentation of an EHIC card for UK residents, contact the post office for latest regulations), although medical insurance is still advised and is essential for all other visitors.

Dental Services As for general medical treatment, nationals of EU countries can obtain dental treatment at a reduced cost, but private medical insurance is still advised for all.

Drugs Prescription and other medicines are available from a pharmacy *(farmacia)*, indicated by a green cross. Pharmacies usually open at the same times as shops (Mon–Sat 8–1, 4–8), and take it in turns to stay open through the afternoon, late evenings and on Sundays.

Safe Water Tap water is safe. So, too, is water from public drinking fountains unless marked *acqua non potabile*.

Staying in Touch

Post Letter boxes are red for normal post and blue for priority post *(posta prioritaria)*. Stamps *(francobolli)* can be bought from post offices, tobacconists showing a 'T' sign and bars. Stamps bought from the private company *globalpostservice* are much more expensive.

Public telephones Public phone boxes seldom exist any more. When ringing from abroad and for local calls the area code or prefix including the '0' must always be dialled as well. Dial 170 for the operator or 12 40 for directory enquiries.

Mobile phones Mobile or cell phones (*telefono cellulare* or the more popular *telefonino*) automatically seek out an appropriate Italian partner network (roaming). The '0' is however not dialled (also applies to calls from abroad). The max. price specified by the EU applies to mobile phone calls. Anyone travelling around Italy for a longer period may find a prepaid chip from the Italian TIM better value. Skype provides cost-free telephoning both within Italy and abroad (www.skype.com).

International Dialling Codes

Dial 011 followed by:

UK:	44
Germany:	49
Ireland:	353
Netherlands:	31
Australia:	61
Spain:	34

WiFi and Internet Most hotels (and many restaurants and bars) have a Wi-Fi connection that can be accessed in all guest rooms and reception areas (sometimes liable to charges)

Emergency Numbers

Police (Polizia di Stato): ☎ 113
Police (Carabinieri): ☎ 112
Children's Emergency Hotline: ☎ 114
Fire: ☎ 115
Ambulance: ☎ 118
Breakdown assistance: ☎ 116

Time

Italy is one hour ahead of GMT in winter, one hour ahead of BST in summer, six hours ahead of New York and nine hours ahead of Los Angeles. Clocks go forward one hour in March and go back in October.

Travel Documents

UK citizens need a passport as do all non-EU citizens. Visitors from most other EU countries only need an identity card. Children must have their own passports or means of identity depending on their age. To bring your own car you will need a **valid driving licence and** the **original vehicle registration form**. A **green card** and original insurance cover note. Although in principle a green card is not needed as Italy is part of the EU, the Italian authorities require one to be carried.

When to Go

Italy is in the **Mediterranean climate zone** (hot, dry summers and wet but mild winters). However, due to Lake Garda's location on the southern edge of the Alps, the summers are not so oppressively hot. There is a pleasant, refreshing wind almost every day. In winter, the lakes act like huge thermal storage reservoirs and take the edge off the chill quite noticeably. Nevertheless, you should always be ready for rainy and foggy weather. Snow in the north of Italy is common, although it only usually settles for any length of time at higher altitudes... with skiing even possible on Monte Baldo.

GETTING THERE

Arriving by Air

Northern Italy has major airports in Turin, Milan and Venice, plus smaller connecting airports across the country. International flights from across Europe also land at smaller airports such as Verona, Bergamo and Brescia.

From the UK, airports are served by Italy's carrier, Alitalia (tel: 087 14 24 14 24, www.alitalia.co.uk), British Airways (tel: 087 08 50 98 50 in UK, 199 71 22 66 in Italy, www.ba.com), bmi baby (tel: 087 12 24 02 24, www.bmibaby.com), easyJet (tel: 087 17 50 01 00, www.easyjet.com), and Ryanair (tel: 087 12 46 00 00, www.ryanair.com). Flying time varies from about 2 to 3½ hours.

From the US, numerous carriers operate direct flights, including Alitalia (tel: 21 29 03 35 75, www.alitliausa.com), American Airlines (tel: 80 04 33 73 00, www.aa.com), Continental (tel: 80 02 31 08 56, www.continental.com), Delta (tel: 80 02 41 41 41, www.delta.com), Northwest Airlines (tel: 80 02 25 25 25, www.nwa.com) and United (tel: 80 05 38 29 29, www.ual.com). Flying time varies from around 11 hours (US west coast) to 8 hours (eastern US).

From the airport to the lake: Buses run from both Verona and Bergamo to Lake Garda but you have to change at the railway station in Verona or Bergamo / Brescia respectively. The journey takes at least one hour and costs around 12 euros. A taxi from Verona Airport to nearby Peschiera costs just under 45 euros; Bergamo Airport to Desenzano costs in the region of 120 euros.

Arriving by Train

Numerous fast and overnight services operate to Milan and Venice from most European capitals, with connections to Bergamo, Brescia and Verona. Motorail services are also available to Verona and Bolzano (from Hamburg for example), to Nice from Calais (leaving just a relatively short drive east to the lakes) and from Denderleeuw (Belgium) to Milan and Venice. See www.trenitalia.it for details. A regular bus service operates from Rovereto and Verona to the lake.

Arriving by Road

By Car: If you are arriving by road you will either cross the Brenner Pass from Innsbruck, following the A22 to northern Lake Garda (exit Rovereto-Sud) and Verona to souther Lake Garda, cross the St Gotthard Pass from Lucerne to reach Lake Lugano and the A9 to Como, or cross the Simplon Pass from the Swiss Valais to reach Domodossola and lakes Orta and Maggiore. If you go into **Switzerland** and drive on the motorways (green signs) you must buy a Swiss motorway tax sticker. To avoid the motorways follow the blue signs to your destination.

Tolls are paid on Italian *autostrade*. Collect a ticket when you get onto the motorway and pay at the booths as you exit.

Arriving By Coach: Eurolines operates long-distance coach services between 31 major European cities, including London, Frankfurt, Hamburg, Milan and Venice.

Flixbus runs a comprehensive and low-priced service to and from several larger cities and even smaller towns in northern Italy (www.flixbus.co.uk).

GETTING AROUND

Driving: Italian roads are excellent. **Sections of the *autostrade*** are two-lane which means they can become congested if slow-moving lorries form convoys. The **lake roads** are good, although care is needed in places, for instance the eastern shore of Lake Maggiore, the road from Como to Bellagio and the parts of the eastern shore of Lake Garda where the roads are narrow. Be careful of **local drivers** travelling at speed and lane discipline can be poor.
The **speed limi**t on *autostrade* is 130kph (80mph). On main roads it is 110kph (70mph), on minor roads 90kph (60mph). In urban areas the limit is 50kph (30mph). The **alcohol limit** is 50 micrograms/100ml. The **Automobile Club Italia (ACI)** operates a **breakdown service**, tel: 800 11 68 00.
Car hire companies can be found at the airports, in Rovereto and larger centres on Lake Garda. In Italy, you must be at least 21 years old to hire a car, have held a driving licence for at least one year and have a credit card. It is generally cheaper to book in advance.
Bus Services: Bus services operate on the **shore roads** of all the major lakes and along the eastern shore of Lake Orta. The services are good, but infrequent on the smaller lakes. On **Lake Garda** bus no. 27 links Riva del Garda with Desenzano del Garda, no. 484 links Riva with Garda, no. 483 Malcesine with Peschiera, while nos. 162–165 and 185 link Garda and Verona. No. 26 runs from Brescia via Desenzano and Sirmione to Verona and back.
Taxis: There are **taxi ranks** in all main towns. They are **expensive** and are not usually a first option for long journeys.
Cycling: The cycle route network on and around Lake Garda is growing slowly but constantly. Most of the tunnels have no lighting so it is imperative to have good lights. Bicycles can also be rented in most tourist centres.
Lake Steamers: All large lakes have **steamer services linking the main towns** (www.navigazionelaghi.it). **Car ferries** operate on Lake Garda with services to the following towns: Toscalano–Maderno and Torri del Benaco and between Limone and Malcesine in summer.

ACCOMMODATION

This guide recommends a cross-section of places to stay. Standards and prices (per room) are comparable with those in other north European countries. Rates may or may not include breakfast (*colazione*). Please note, that many hotels on the lake are only open in the summer season between Easter and October.

FOOD & DRINK

Italian cooking is one of the great joys of travelling to this country. As a general rule, whatever standard of restaurant you choose the food will be both well cooked and well presented.
The difference between a *pizzeria*, a *trattoria* and a *ristorante* is sometimes blurred. In general, ***pizzerie*** are inexpensive and serve a variety of pizzas, some pasta dishes and there may well be a salad bar, too. ***Trattorie*** have more extensive dishes, but both the menu and the food will be 'no frills'. It will, however, be well prepared and well served. ***Ristoranti*** tend to offer the greatest choice. ***Osteria*** and ***locanda*** are country inns or guesthouses.
Restaurants to suit different budgets are listed in this guidebook according to region in the respective chapters.
Most restaurants add ***pane e coperto*** (bread and cover) to the bill. It is normal to **add a tip** as well as paying the *coperto*.
Bars are something special in Italy: lots of Italians have a quick breakfast in a bar (a croissant and a cup of coffee) and stop by for an *espresso* during the day. Standing at the bar is known as *al banco*; prices are higher if you sit down. In bars it is usual to pay for your drink first at the cash desk. The cashier will give you a **purchase ticket** which you then hand to the waiter behind the bar who will make your drink.

Drinks

Italians generally drink an **espresso** or a **cappuccino** in the morning accompanied by a croissant (*un cornetto*). After lunch or dinner they only ever order an espresso, never a cappuccino.

Tea (*un tè nero*) is still something rather exotic for most Italians. And when they drink tea it is always with a slice of lemon (*un tè al limone*). If you want tea with milk, order a *tè con latte*, or better still *con latte freddo* (with cold milk).

Mineral water (*acqua minerale*) is drunk by many Italians at meals: sparkling water (*acqua gassata*) or still (*acqua non gassata*). Italians often drink a light open **wine** with their meal (*vino sfuso/vino della casa*) – generally speaking such wines are good and cheap as well as dry, of course.

Beer (*birra*) is generally a light lager; there are however also ***dunkel* beers** (*birra scura, nera* or *rossa*). Just ask for a draught beer (*birra alla spina*). Good Italian brews are Peroni and Nastro Azzurro.

Standard **aperitifs** include Martini, Cinzano, Campari and Aperol Spritz. If you order Campari Soda you will be served a pre-prepared product from a bottle; real Campari Soda is called Bitter Campari. Prosecco from Veneto is also very popular. After dinner, **brandy** is often drunk (Vecchia Romagna is the best), *limoncello* (lemon liqueur) or *amaro* (herbal liqueur). Averna is considered one of the best brands. *Grappa*, a strong, grape-based pomace brandy, is also served as a **digestif** as is the sweet almond liqueur *amaretto*. The aniseed brandy *sambuca* is traditionally served with coffee beans.

Types of coffee

un espresso (or, more frequently, **un caffè**) – strong, black coffee served in small cups
un doppio caffè/espresso – a double espresso
un lungo – an espresso made with more water
un macchiato – an espresso with a spoonful of foamed milk
un caffè corretto – espresso with a shot of liqueur or schnaps
un cappuccino – an espresso with foamed milk (never with cream!)
un caffè latte – an espresso with much more milk without the foam
un americano – a cup of filter coffee
un caffè Hag – decaffeinated coffee
un caffè freddo – an iced coffee, generally already (generously) sweetened; if you want one without sugar ask for *un amaro*.
un cappuccino freddo – a chilled milk coffee

ENTERTAINMENT

'In' places come and go but the clubs near Desenzano and in Bardolino are especially popular. You can also enjoy the evenings on Lake Garda without spectacular laser or thunderous sound shows. In high season, the lakeside promenades and the Old Towns are atmospherically lit up. Musicians and bands perform on the streets and squares, buskers show off their talents and restaurant owners are only to happy to serve their customers under the stars until midnight. There are many open-air parties, pop and rock concerts and firework displays. Several tips are listed in this guidebook in each of the chapters on the different regions.

FESTIVALS & EVENTS

January

On 1.1. at 3pm the traditional **New Year's swim** in the lake takes place in Magugnano (Brenzone) – irrespective of what the weather is like or how cold the water.

February

Festa di Mezzaquaresima: This festival is held three weeks before Easter, in the middle of Lent, in Limone. It's not regarded as breaking the fast – religious Christians continue to go without meat – but there is any quantity of fish. And as these 'need to swim', white wine is consumed as well!

June

Festa del Nodo d'Amore: Tortellini were allegedly invented in Valeggio. For this reason the 600m (1968ft)-long Visconti Bridge is turned into one huge open-air restaurant on the third Tuesday in June. 4000 people come to celebrate the Festa del Nodo d'Amore on the bridge where more than 600,000 *nodi d'amore* – 'love knots' – as tortellini are called in Valeggio, are served.

June–September
Malcesine e l'Europa: Concerts are held in the summer and plays performed on the beautifully located open-air stage near the castle with its magnificent backdrop.

July
Regatta Bisse: A late-evening boat race at the southern end of Lake Garda, starting in Bardolino. In keeping with the tradition of the Venetian Republic, the often beautiful old boats are rowed standing. The historical competition is preceded by a procession of flag throwers. In summer, when the water is calm, you can watch people training for the rowing competition in virtually all towns and villages around the lake.

July/August
The Verona Opera Festival in Verona.

August
Notte di San Lorenzo: 10 August is a very special night when it 'rains' shooting stars. The whole of Italy gaze's at the night sky and, in Peschiera, a big folk festival is staged during the meteor shower.
Palio delle Contrade is the name of a competition between the different districts of Garda with a canoe race held every year in the evening on 15 August. The teams comprise four rowers to a boat, just like the crews of old in boats used for transporting things and for fishing. The winners of this traditional race with Venetian roots celebrate with a fireworks display.
Notte d'Incanto: Also on **Ferragosto** (15 August) thousands of floating lights and candles bob around on the lake during the 'night of magic'.

September
Centomiglia: The 'Hundred Mile Regatta' (Centomiglia) starts from the marina in Bogliaco (Gargnano).
Rock Master: The international free-climbing championship is held every year in September near Arco.

September/October
Festa dell'Uva: For more than 60 years a big wine festival has been held on the harbour and lakeside promenade at Bardolino in autumn – the perfect occasion to taste the various Bardolino wines! After dark, there is a fireworks display.

November
Santa Caterina Day: A large festival is held in Castelletto di Brenzone after the olives have been harvested and the first drops of the new oil (*olio novello*) have started to flow from the oil presses. You can sample and buy cold-pressed *extra vergine* oil directly from the producers themselves.

SHOPPING

Leather is an Italian speciality – shoes, handbags and jackets being of the highest quality. Bardolino and Valpolicella in the east and Franciacorta in the west are famous **wine-growing** areas, and Lake Garda especially is famous for its **olive oil**.
Opening hours: Most shops are open from 9am–1pm and from 3pm–8pm, In the tourist centres, especially in the high season, the opening hours are often longer, often without a lunch break and sometimes even open seven days a week. Otherwise shops are generally closed on Sun. Several **shopping tips** and the **market days** of some towns and villages are listed in this guidebook in each of the chapters on the different regions.
Bergamo (Bergamo Alto pedestrian precinct): typical fleamarket with all sorts of things every 3rd Sun in the month (except Aug), **Brescia** (Piazza della Vittoria): every 2nd second Sun of each month (except in July and Aug); especially good for antiques, furniture and objets d'art. Other specialist markets can be found in: **Cremona** (Via Dante Alighieri, every 3rd Sun of each month, well-known for furniture and objets d'art), **Mantua** (Piazza Castello, every 3rd Sun of each month, good for antiques), **Varese** (Piazza Montegrappa, every 1st Sun of each month, good for antiques and objets d'art) und **Verona** (Porta Palio, every 1st Sun of each month, good for antiques, objets d'art and crafts).

USEFUL WORDS AND PHRASES

Survival Phrases

yes / no	**sì / non**
please	**per favore**
thank you	**grazie**
you're welcome	**di niente / prego**
I'm sorry	**mi dispiace**
goodbye	**arrivederci**
good morning	**buongiorno**
goodnight	**buona sera**
how are you?	**come sta?**
how much?	**quanto costa?**
I would like...	**vorrei...**
open / closed	**aperto / chiuso**
today / tomorrow	**oggi / domani**
Monday / Tuesday	**lunedì / martedì**
Wednesday	**mercoledì**
Thursday / Friday	**giovedì / venerdì**
Saturday / Sunday	**sabato / domenica**

Directions

I'm lost	**mi sono perso/a**
Where is ...?	**dove si trova ...?**
... the station	**... la stazione**
... the telephone	**... il telefono**
... the bank	**... la banca**
... the toilet	**... il bagno**
turn left	**volti a sinistra**
turn right	**volti a destra**
go straight on	**vada dritto**
at the corner	**all'angolo**
the street	**la strada**
the building	**il palazzo**
the traffic light	**il semaforo**
the crossroads	**l'incrocio**
the signs for ...	**le indicazione per ...**

If you need help

Help!	**Aiuto!**
Could you help me, please?	**Mi potrebbe aiutare?**
Do you speak English?	**Parla inglese?**
I don't understand	**Non capisco**
Please could you call a doctor quickly?	**Mi chiami presto un medico, per favore?**

Restaurant

I'd like to book a table	**Vorrei prenotare un tavolo**
A table for two please	**Un tavolo per due, per favore**
Could we see the menu, please?	**Ci porta la lista, per favore?**
What's this?	**Cosa è questo?**
A bottle of / a glass of...	**Un bottiglia di / un bicchiere di...**
Could I have the bill?	**Ci porta il conto?**

Accommodation

Do you have a single / double room?	**Ha una camera singola / doppia?**
with / without	**con/senza**
bath / toilet / shower	**vasca / gabinetto / doccia**
Does that include breakfast?	**E'inclusa la prima colazione?**
Does that include dinner?	**E'inclusa la cena?**
Do you have room service?	**C'è il servizio in camera?**
Could I see the room?	**E' possibile vedere la camera?**
I'll take this room	**Prendo questa**
Thanks for your hospitality	**Grazie per l'ospitalità**

Numbers

0	**zero**
1	**una / uno**
2	**due**
3	**tre**
4	**quattro**
5	**cinque**
6	**sei**
7	**sette**
8	**otto**
9	**nove**
10	**dieci**
11	**undici**
12	**dodici**
13	**tredici**
14	**quattordici**
15	**quindici**

16	**sedici**
17	**diciassette**
18	**diciotto**
19	**diciannove**
20	**venti**
21	**ventuno**
22	**ventidue**
30	**trenta**
40	**quaranta**
50	**cinquanta**
60	**sessanta**
70	**settanta**
80	**ottanta**
90	**novanta**
100	**cento**
101	**centouno**
110	**centodieci**
120	**centoventi**
200	**duecento**
300	**trecento**
400	**quattrocento**
500	**cinquecento**
600	**seicento**
700	**settecento**
800	**ottocento**
900	**novecento**
1,000	**mille**
2,000	**duemila**
10,000	**diecimila**
1,000,000	**un milione**
½	**mezza/mezzo**
⅓	**un terzo**
¼	**un quatro**
¾	**tre quarti**

Menu Reader

acciuga	anchovy
acqua	water
affettati	sliced cured meats
affumicato	smoked
aglio	garlic
agnello	lamb
anatra	duck
antipasti	hors d'oeuvres
arista	roast pork
arrosto	roast
asparagi	asparagus
birra	beer
bistecca	steak
bollito	boiled meat
braciola	minute steak
brasato	braised
brodo	broth
bruschetta	toasted bread with garlic or tomato topping
budino	pudding
burro	butter
cacciagione	game
cacciatore, alla	rich tomato sauce with mushrooms
caffè corretto	coffee with liqueur / spirit
caffè macchiato	coffee with a drop of milk
caffè freddo	iced coffee
caffè latte	milky coffee
caffè lungo	weak coffee
caffè ristretto	strong coffee
calamaro	squid
cappero	caper
carciofo	artichoke
carota	carrot
carne	meat
carpa	carp
casalingo	homemade
cassata	Sicilian fruit ice cream
cavolfiore	cauliflower
cavolo	cabbage
ceci	chickpeas
cervello	brains
cervo	venison
cetriolino	gherkin
cetriolo	cucumber
cicoria	chicory
cinghiale	boar
cioccolata	chocolate
cipolla	onion
coda di bue	oxtail
coniglio	rabbit
contorni	vegetables
coperto	cover charge
coscia	leg of meat
cotolette	cutlets
cozze	mussels
crema	custard
crostini	canape with savoury toppings or croutons

crudo	raw
digestivo	after-dinner liqueur
dolci	cakes / desserts
erbe aromatiche	herbs
facito	stuffed
fagioli	beans
fagiolini	green beans
faraona	guinea fowl
fegato	liver
finocchio	fennel
formaggio	cheese
forno, al	baked
frittata	omelette
fritto	fried
frizzante	fizzy
frulatto	whisked
frutta	fruit
frutti di mare	seafood
funghi	mushrooms
gamberetto	shrimp
gelato	ice cream
ghiaccio	ice
gnocchi	potato dumplings
granchio	crab
gran(o)turco	corn
griglia, alla	grilled
imbottito	stuffed
insalata	salad
IVA	VAT
latte	milk
lepre	hare
lumache	snails
manzo	beef
merluzzo	cod
miele	honey
minestra	soup
molluschi	shellfish
olio	oil
oliva	olive
ostrica	oyster
pancetta	bacon
pane	bread
panino	roll
panna	cream
parmigiano	Parmesan
passata	sieved or creamed
pastasciutta	dried pasta cooked with sauce
pasta sfoglia	puff pastry
patate fritte	chips
pecora	mutton
pecorino	sheep's milk cheese
peperoncino	chilli
peperone	red / green pepper
pesce	fish
petto	breast
piccione	pigeon
piselli	peas
pollame	fowl
pollo	chicken
polpetta	meatball
pomodori	tomatoes
porto	port wine
pranzo	lunch
prezzemolo	parsley
primo piatto	first course
prosciutto cotto	cooked ham
prosciutto crudo	dry-cured ham
ragù	meat sauce
ripieno	stuffed
riso	rice
salsa	sauce
salsiccia	sausage
saltimbocca	veal with prosciutto and sage
sarde	sardines
secco	dry
secondo piatto	main course
senape	mustard
servizio compreso	service charge included
sogliola	sole
spuntini	snacks
succa di frutta	fruit juice
sugo	sauce
tonno	tuna
uovo affrogato / in carnica	poached egg
uovo al tegamo / fritto	fried egg
uovo alla coque	soft boiled egg
uovo alla sodo	hard boiled egg
uova strapazzate	scambled egg
verdure	vegetables
vino bianco	white wine
vino rosato	rosé wine
vino rosso	red wine
vitello	veal
zucchero	sugar
zucchino	courgette
zuppa	soup

Road Atlas

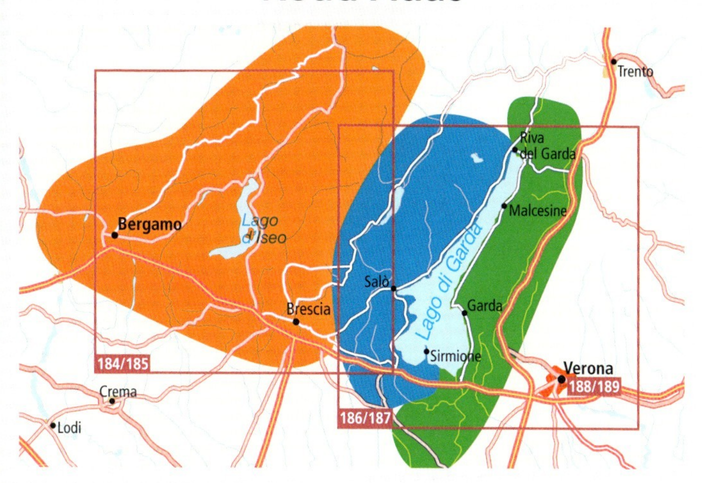

Key to Road Atlas

A14 2	Motorway
E 55	Dual carriageway
SS16	Trunk road
	Main road
	Secondary road
	Road under construction/development
	Tunnel
	Railroad
	Ferry
	International, province boundary
	National park, National preserve
	Restricted area
2 ★★	Top 10
11	Don't Miss
12	At Your Leisure

	International airport
	Regional airport
	Monastery / Church, chapel
	Castle, fortress / Ruin
★	Point of interest
	Archaeological site
	Tower / Lighthouse
	Waterfall / Cave, grotto
	Mountain peak / Pass
	Campground / Lookout point
	Information / Hospital
M	Museum / Theatre, opera house
	Police / Post office
	Harbour, mooring / (Swimming) beach
P P	Multi-storey / Parking

1 : 360 000

0 10 20km

0 5 10mi

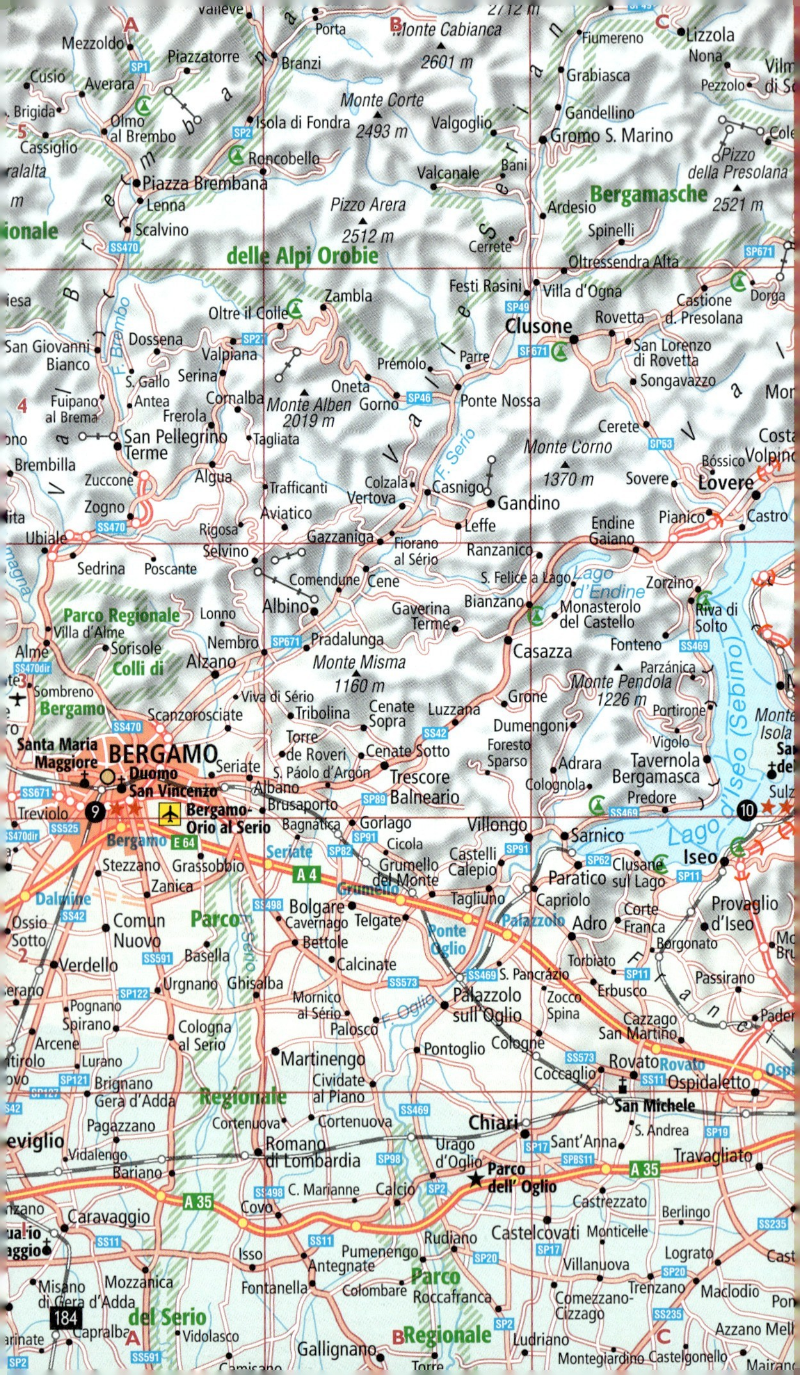
A
B
C
5
4
3
2
1
Valleve
Porta
Monte Cabianca
2601 m
2712 m
Fiumenero
Lizzola
Nona
Pezzolo
Mezzoldo
Piazzatorre
Branzi
SP1
Cusio
Averara
Brigida
Olmo al Brembo
Isola di Fondra
Monte Corte
2493 m
Valgoglio
Grabiasca
Gandellino
Gromo S. Marino
Cassiglio
SP2
Roncobello
Bani
Pizzo della Presolana
2521 m
Piazza Brembana
Lenna
Scalvino
Valcanale
Pizzo Arera
2512 m
Cerrete
Ardesio
Bergamasche
Spinelli
SS470
delle Alpi Orobie
Oltressendra Alta
SP671
Festi Rasini
Villa d'Ogna
Zambla
Castione d. Presolana
Dorga
Oltre il Colle
SP49
Clusone
Rovetta
F. Brembo
San Giovanni Bianco
Dossena
SP27
Valpiana
Parre
San Lorenzo di Rovetta
Songavazzo
S. Gallo
Serina
Prémolo
Oneta
Gorno
SP46
Ponte Nossa
Fuipiano al Brema
Antea
Cornalba
Monte Alben
2019 m
Frerola
San Pellegrino Terme
Tagliata
Cerete
SP53
F. Serio
Monte Corno
1370 m
Bóssico
Volpino
Brembilla
Zuccone
Algua
Trafficanti
Colzala
Vertova
Casnigo
Gandino
Sovere
Lovere
Zogno
SS470
Aviatico
Leffe
Pianico
Castro
Ubiale
Rigosa
Gazzaniga
Fiorano al Sério
Ranzanico
Endine Gaiano
Sedrina
Poscante
Selvino
Comendune
Cene
S. Felice a Lago
Lago d'Endine
Zorzino
Monasterolo del Castello
Bianzano
Gaverina Terme
Riva di Solto
Parco Regionale
Lonno
Albino
Villa d'Almè
Almè
Sorisole
Nembro
Pradalunga
SP671
Casazza
Fonteno
SS469
SS470dir
Colli di
Alzano
Monte Misma
1160 m
Parzánica
Monte Pendola
1226 m
Sombreno
Bergamo
Viva di Sério
Tribolina
Cenate Sopra
Luzzana
Grone
Portirone
Monte Isola
Lago d'Iseo (Sebino)
Scanzorosciate
SS470
SS42
Dumengoni
Torre de Roveri
Foresto Sparso
Vigolo
Santa Maria Maggiore
BERGAMO
Duomo
San Vincenzo
Seriate
Cenate Sotto
Adrara
Tavernola Bergamasca
S. Pàolo d'Argón
Trescore Balneario
Albano
Colognola
Predore
SS671
Treviolo
9
Bergamo-Orio al Serio
Brusaporto
SP89
SS469
10
Sulz
SS525
SS470dir
Bagnatica
Gorlago
Villongo
Sarnico
Bergamo
E 64
Seriate
SP91
Cicola
Castelli Calepio
SP91
Lago d'Iseo
Iseo
SP82
Grumello del Monte
SP62
Clusane sul Lago
Stezzano
Grassobbio
Paratico
SP11
Zanica
A 4
Grumello
Tagliuno
Capriolo
Dalmine
SS498
Bolgare
Cavernago
Telgate
Corte Franca
Provaglio d'Iseo
Ossio Sotto
SS42
Comun Nuovo
Parco
F. Serio
Palazzolo
Adro
Ponte Oglio
Bettole
Borgonato
Verdello
SS591
Basella
Calcinate
Torbiato
Ghisalba
SS469
S. Pancràzio
SP11
Passirano
SP122
Urgnano
SS573
Palazzolo sull'Oglio
Zocco Spina
Erbusco
Pognano
Mornico al Sério
F. Oglio
Spirano
Palosco
Cazzago San Martino
Arcene
Cologna al Serio
Cologne
Lurano
Martinengo
Pontoglio
SS573
Rovato
Rovato
SP121
Brignano
Cividate al Piano
Coccaglio
SS11
Ospidaletto
SP127
Gera d'Adda
Regionale
San Michele
SS469
Pagazzano
Cortenuova
Cortenuova
Chiari
S. Andrea
SP19
Treviglio
Vidalengo
Romano di Lombardia
SP98
Urago d'Oglio
SP17
Sant'Anna
Travagliato
Bariano
SP8S11
Parco dell' Oglio
A 35
SS498
C. Marianne
Calcio
SP2
A 35
Caravaggio
Covo
Castrezzato
Berlingo
Rudiano
Castelcovati
Monticelle
SS235
SS11
SS11
Pumenengo
SP20
SP17
Lograto
Isso
Antegnate
Villanuova
SP20
Parco
Misano di Gera d'Adda
Mozzanica
Fontanella
Colombare
Roccafranca
Trenzano
Maclodio
Comezzano-Cizzago
SS235
184
del Serio
SP2
Capralba
Vidolasco
Regionale
Ludriano
Azzano Mella
SS591
SP2
Gallignano
Torre
Montegiardino
Castelgonnello
Mairano

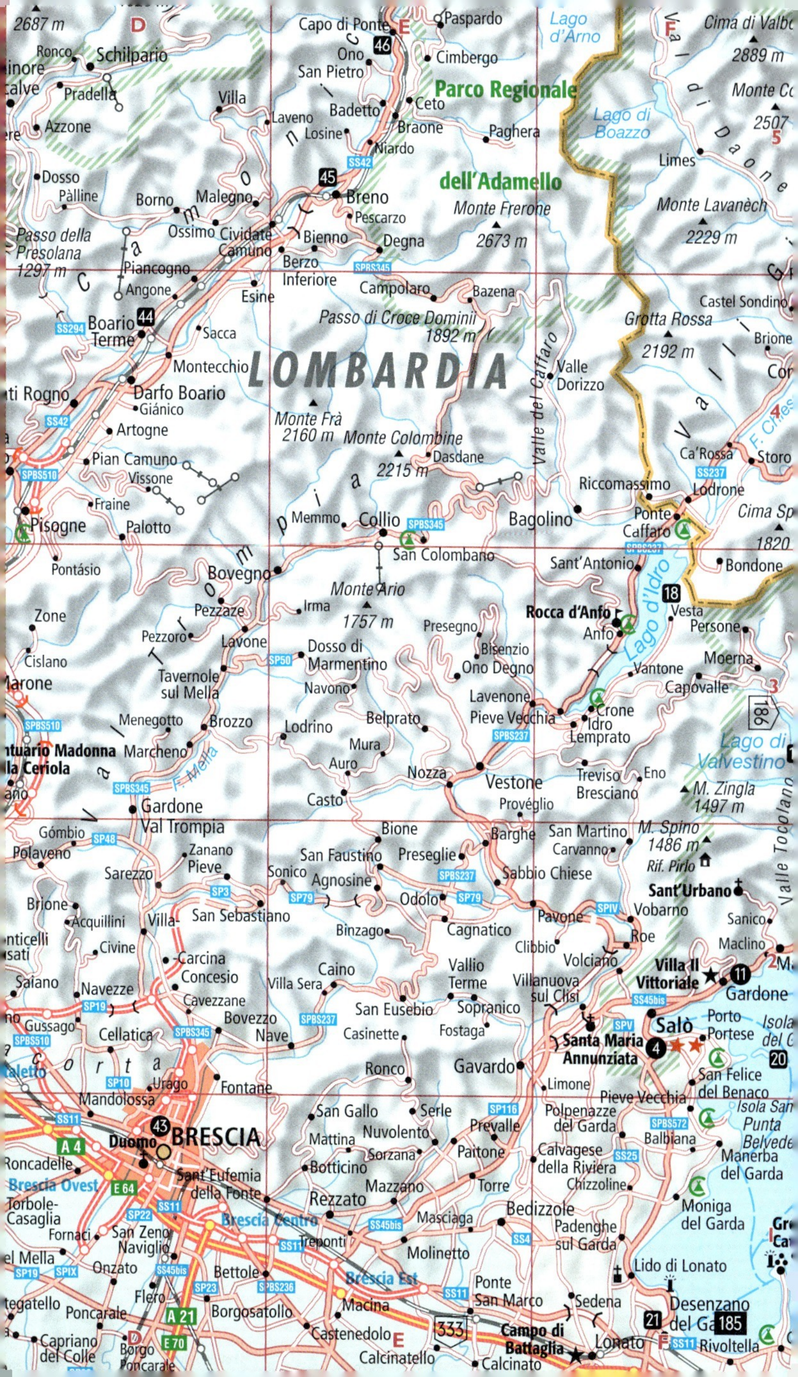
2687 m
D
Ronco
Schilpario
Pradella
Azzone
Villa
Laveno
Losine
Capo di Ponte
E
46
Ono
San Pietro
Badetto
Ceto
Braone
Niardo
SS42
Paspardo
Cimbergo
Parco Regionale
dell'Adamello
Paghera
Lago d'Arno
Lago di Boazzo
F
Cima di Valbo
2889 m
Monte Co
2507
5
Limes
Val di Daone
Monte Lavanèch
2229 m
Dosso
Pàlline
Borno
Malegno
45
Breno
Pescarzo
Monte Frerone
2673 m
Passo della Presolana
1297 m
Ossimo
Cividate Camuno
Bienno
Berzo Inferiore
Degna
SPBS345
Piancogno
Angone
Esine
Campolaro
Bazena
Boario Terme
44
SS294
Sacca
Passo di Croce Domini
1892 m
Castel Sondino
Grotta Rossa
2192 m
Brione
LOMBARDIA
Montecchio
Valle del Caffaro
Valle Dorizzo
Rogno
Darfo Boario
Giánico
Artogne
SS42
Monte Frà
2160 m
Monte Colombine
2215 m
Dasdade
Val
4
F. Chiese
Ca'Rossa
Storo
SS237
Pian Camuno
Vissone
SPBS510
Fraine
Pisogne
Palotto
Memmo
Collio
SPBS345
San Colombano
Bagolino
Riccomassimo
Lodrone
Ponte Caffaro
Cima Sp
1820
Sant'Antonio
Bondone
Pontásio
Bovegno
Monte Ario
1757 m
18
Rocca d'Anfo
Anfo
Lago d'Idro
Vesta
Persone
Zone
Pezzaze
Irma
Presegno
Pezzoro
Lavone
Bisenzio
Cislano
Marone
SP50
Dosso di Marmentino
Ono Degno
Vantone
Moerna
Capovalle
3
Tavernole sul Mella
Navono
Lavenone
Crone
Idro
Lemprato
186
SPBS510
Menegotto
Brozzo
Lodrino
Belprato
Pieve Vecchia
SPBS237
Lago di Valvestino
Santuario Madonna della Ceriola
Marcheno
F. Mella
Mura
Auro
Nozza
Vestone
Treviso Bresciano
Eno
M. Zingla
1497 m
SPBS345
Casto
Provéglio
Gardone Val Trompia
Val Trompia
Gómbio
SP48
Bione
Barghe
San Martino
M. Spino
1486 m
Carvanno
Rif. Pirlo
Valle Toscolano
Polaveno
Zanano
Pieve
San Faustino
Preseglie
Sarezzo
Sonico
Agnosine
SPBS237
Sabbio Chiese
Sant'Urbano
SP3
SP79
Odolo
SP79
Brione
Acquillini
Villa
San Sebastiano
Pavone
SPIV
Vobarno
Sanico
Binzago
Cagnatico
Roe
Civine
Clibbio
Maclino
Carcina
Caino
Vallio Terme
Volciano
Villa Il Vittoriale
11
Concesio
Villa Sera
Villanuova sul Clisi
Gardone
Saiano
Navezze
Cavezzane
San Eusebio
Sopranico
SS45bis
SP19
Bovezzo
SPBS237
SPV
Salò
Porto Portese
Gussago
Nave
Casinette
Fostaga
Santa Maria Annunziata
4
SPBS510
Cellatica
SPBS345
Isola del G
20
Franciacorta
Ronco
Gavardo
San Felice del Benaco
SP10
Urago
Fontane
Limone
Mandolossa
Pieve Vecchia
Polpenazze del Garda
Isola San
Punta Belvede
SS11
San Gallo
Serle
SP116
Prevalle
43
BRESCIA
SPBS572
Balbiana
A 4
Duomo
Mattina
Nuvolento
Paitone
Calvagese della Riviera
SS25
Manerba del Garda
Sorzana
Roncadelle
Botticino
Brescia Ovest
E 64
Sant'Eufemia della Fonte
Mazzano
Torre
Chizzoline
Torbole-Casaglia
SS11
Rezzato
Moniga del Garda
SP22
Brescia Centro
Bedizzole
Masciaga
SS45bis
Padenghe sul Garda
Fornaci
San Zeno Naviglio
Treponti
SS4
SS11
Molinetto
Mella
Onzato
SP19
SPIX
SS45bis
Bettole
Brescia Est
Lido di Lonato
SP23
SPBS236
Ponte San Marco
Flero
SS11
Sedena
Desenzano del Garda
tegatello
Poncarale
A 21
Borgosatollo
Macina
21
185
333
Campo di Battaglia
Lonato
F
SS11
Rivoltella
Castenedolo
E
Capriano del Colle
D
Borgo Poncarale
E 70
Calcinatello
Calcinato

LOMBARDIA
Inferiore
Campolaro
Bazena
Passo di Croce Domini 1892 m
333
Grotta Rossa 2192 m
Castel Sondino
Cimego
Brione
Condino
Tiarno-di-Sotto
Tiarno-di-Sopra
Bezzecca
Lago di Ledro
Lago di Ampola
F. Chiese
Valle Dorizzo
Valle del Caffaro
Monte Frà 2160 m
Monte Colombine 2215 m
Dasdane
Ca'Rossa
Storo
SS237
SS240
Val d'Ampola
Monte Tremalzo 1974 m
Passo di Tremalzo 1694 m
Cima Spessa 1820 m
Riccomassimo
Lodrone
Ponte Caffaro
Memmo
Collio
SPBS345
San Colombano
Bagolino
Sant'Antonio
SPBS237
Bondone
Parco Regionale
Tremosine
Monte Ario 1757 m
Irma
Presegno
Rocca d'Anfo
Anfo
Lago d'Idro
Vesta
Persone
Magasa
Cádria
dell' Alto
Dosso di Marmentino
SP50
Bisenzio
Ono Degno
Vantone
Moerna
Capovalle
Bresciano
Pieve
Campione del Garda
Navono
Lavenone
Pieve Vecchia
Crone
Idro
Lemprato
Tignale
Lodrino
Belprato
Mura
Auro
Lago di Valvestino
Costa
Piovere
Oldesio
Briano
185
Nozza
Vestone
Treviso Bresciano
Eno
M. Zingla 1497 m
Brenzone
Casto
Provéglio
Valle Tocolano
Gargnano
SS45bis
Bione
Barghe
San Martino
Carvanno
M. Spino 1486 m
Rif. Pirlo
Villa
Villa Bettoni
Castelletto di Brenzone
San Faustino
Preseglie
Sabbio Chiese
Bogliaco
Sonico
Agnosine
SPBS237
Sant'Urbano
Gaino
Odolo
SP79
Vobarno
Sanico
Toscolano
Pai
Pavone
SPIV
Roe
Crero
Binzago
Cagnatico
Clibbio
Maclino
Maderno
Volciano
Caino
Vallio Terme
Villa Il Vittoriale
Gardone Riviera
Villa Sera
Villanuova sul Clisi
Torri del Benaco
Monte Luppia 418 m
San Eusebio
Sopranico
SS45bis
Salò
Porto Portese
Isola del Garda
Acque Fredde
Nave
Casinette
Fostaga
Santa Maria Annunziata
SPV
Ronco
Gavardo
San Felice del Benaco
San Vigilio
Garda
Punta San Vigilio
Limone
Pieve Vecchia
Isola San Biagio
San Gallo
Serle
SP116
Polpenazze del Garda
Punta Belvedere
Mattina
Nuvolento
Prevalle
SPBS572
Balbiana
Bardolino
Sorzana
Paitone
Calvagese della Riviera
SS25
Manerba del Garda
Botticino
Chizzoline
Cavaion Veronese
Rezzato
Mazzano
Torre
Moniga del Garda
Cisano
Masciaga
Bedizzole
Padenghe sul Garda
Grotte di Catullo
Madonna delle Pergolana
Brescia Centro
SS45bis
SS4
Sirmione
Lazise
Treponti
Molinetto
Lido di Lonato
Brescia Est
SS11
Ponte San Marco
Sedena
Desenzano del Garda
SPBS236
Macina
Campo di Battaglia
Lonato
SS11
Rivoltella
Colombare
Fossalta
Castenedolo
Gardaland
Calcinatello
Calcinato
SS11
Lugana
Pacengo
Desenzano
SS343
SS567
Le Tassere
SR11
Peschiera del Garda
Vighizzolo
Brescia-Montichiari G. d'Annunzio
Centenaro
A 4
E 70
Sirmione
SR450
Montichiari
Esenta
Castel Venzago
San Martino della Battaglia
Madonna del Frassino
Peschiera
Ponti sul Mincio
SP13
Abbazia di San Vigilio
SPBS236
SS567
Pozzolengo
SP19
Salionze
Case Oriani
Novagli
SPBS668
SP27
F. Chiese
Castiglione delle Stiviere
Castellaro Lagusello
SR249
Monzambano
SP8
Malpaga
SS343
Pozzo Catena
Solferino
Parco Giardino Sigurtà
186
Calvisano
Mezzane
Carpenedolo
San Cassiano
Borghetto
SS343
S. Vigilio
SP8
SS236
Cavriana
Campagnolo
SP20

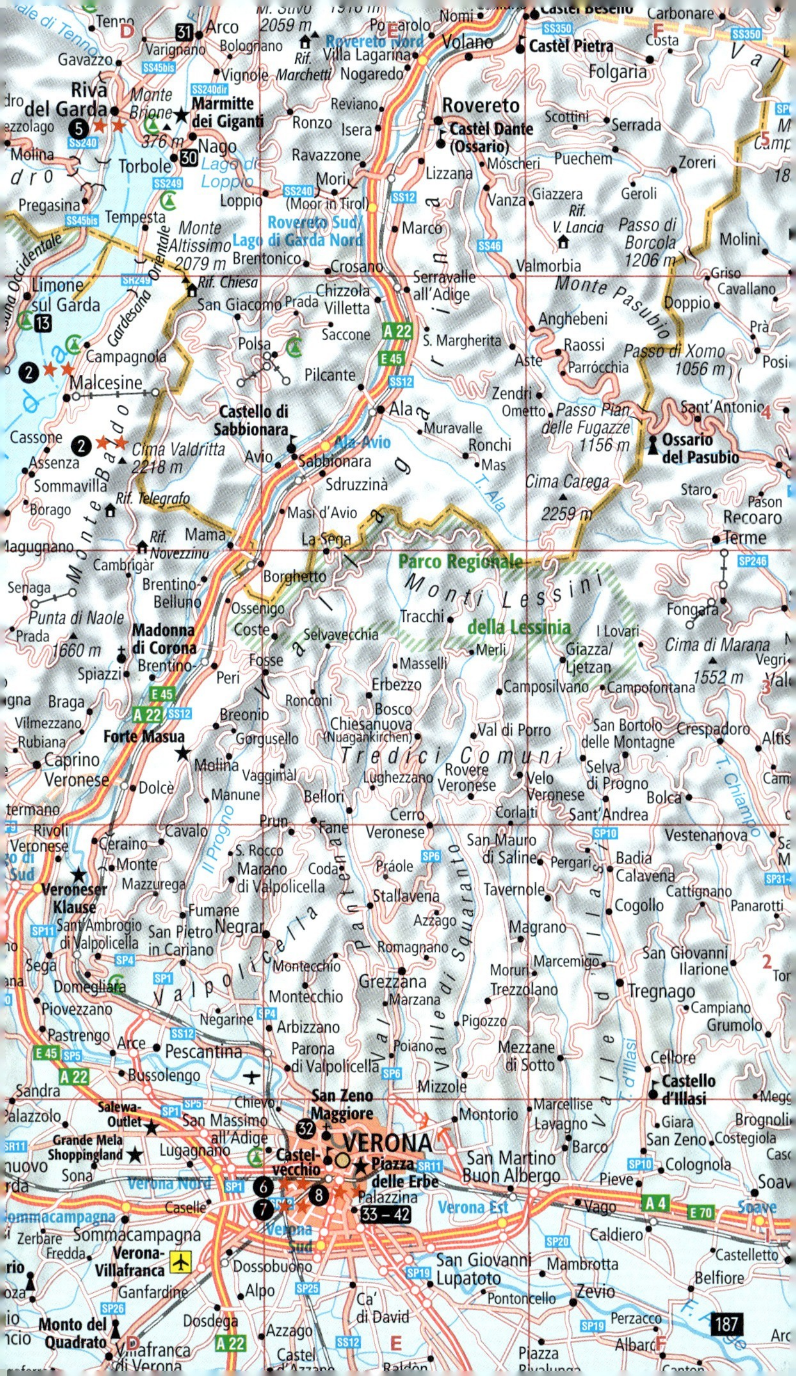

Tenno
D
31
Arco
M. Stivo
2059 m
Rif. Marchetti
Pomarolo
E
Nomi
Castel Beseno
Carbonare
F
Gavazzo
Varignano
Bolognano
Rovereto Nord
Villa Lagarina
Volano
Castèl Pietra
Costa
Folgaria
SS45bis
SS350
Vignole
Nogaredo
Riva del Garda
Monte Brione
376 m
Marmitte dei Giganti
Ronzo
Reviano
Isera
Rovereto
Castèl Dante (Ossario)
Scottini
Serrada
5
Molina
Torbole
Nago
30
Lago di Loppio
Ravazzone
Mori
Lizzana
Moscheri
Puechem
Zoreri
Loppio
(Moor in Tirol)
SS240
SS12
Vanza
Giazzera
Rif. V. Lancia
Geroli
Pregasina
Tempesta
Rovereto Sud/ Lago di Garda Nord
Marco
SS46
Passo di Borcola
1206 m
Molini
Monte Altissimo
2079 m
Brentonico
Crosano
Valmorbia
Griso
Cavallano
Limone sul Garda
Rif. Chiesa
San Giacomo
Prada
Chizzola
Villetta
Serravalle all'Adige
Monte Pasubio
Doppio
13
Gardesana Orientale
Saccone
A 22
S. Margherita
Anghebeni
Raossi
Prà
Campagnola
Polsa
E 45
Aste
Parrócchia
Passo di Xomo
1056 m
Posina
2
Malcesine
Pilcante
SS12
Zendri
Ometto
Ala
Sant'Antonio
4
Castello di Sabbionara
Passo Pian delle Fugazze
1156 m
Cassone
Cima Valdritta
2218 m
Muravalle
Ossario del Pasubio
Assenza
Avio
Ala-Avio
Ronchi
Mas
Sommavilla
Sabbionara
Sdruzzinà
Cima Carega
2259 m
Staro
Pason
Rif. Telegrafo
Borago
Masi d'Avio
T. Ala
Recoaro Terme
Monte Baldo
Mama
La Sega
Rif. Novezzino
Magugnano
Cambrigàr
Parco Regionale
SP246
Borghetto
Senaga
Brentino-Belluno
Monti Lessini
Ossenigo
Tracchi
Fongara
Punta di Naole
1660 m
Madonna di Corona
Coste
della Lessinia
I Lovari
Prada
Selvavecchia
Merli
Giazza/ Ljetzan
Cima di Marana
1552 m
Brentino
Fosse
Masselli
Spiazzi
Peri
Vegri
Erbezzo
Camposilvano
Campofontana
3
Braga
E 45
Ronconi
Bosco Chiesanuova
(Nuaganklrchen)
A 22
SS12
Breonio
San Bortolo delle Montagne
Crespadoro
Vilmezzano
Forte Masua
Val di Porro
Rubiana
Gorgusello
Caprino Veronese
Tredici Comuni
Molina
Lughezzano
Rovere Veronese
Velo Veronese
Selva di Progno
T. Chiampo
Vaggimàl
Dolcè
Bolca
Manune
Bellori
Corlaiti
Sant'Andrea
Rivoli Veronese
Prun
Fane
Cerro Veronese
SP10
Vestenanova
Cavalo
San Mauro di Saline
Ceraino
S. Rocco
Coda
SP6
Pergari
Badia Calavena
Monte
Marano di Valpolicella
Pràole
Il Progno
Veroneser Klause
Mazzurega
Stallavena
Tavernole
Cattignano
Panarotti
Fumane
Val Pantena
Cogollo
SP11
Sant'Ambrogio di Valpolicella
San Pietro in Cariano
Negrar
Azzago
Valle di Squaranto
Magrano
Romagnano
Marcemigo
San Giovanni Ilarione
Sega
SP4
Montecchio
Moruri
Grezzana
Domegliara
SP1
Valpolicella
Trezzolano
Tregnago
Montecchio
Marzana
Campiano
2
Piovezzano
Negarine
SP4
Arbizzano
Pigozzo
Valle d'Illasi
Grumolo
Pastrengo
SS12
Arce
Pescantina
Parona di Valpolicella
Poiano
Mezzane di Sotto
Cellore
E 45
SP5
T. d'Illasi
A 22
Bussolengo
Castello d'Illasi
Sandra
SP6
Mizzole
Chievo
San Zeno Maggiore
Marcellise
Palazzolo
Salewa-Outlet
SP5
Montorio
Lavagno
Giara
Brognoligo
San Massimo all'Adige
32
Grande Mela Shoppingland
VERONA
Barco
San Zeno
Costegiola
Lugagnano
Castel-vecchio
Piazza delle Erbe
San Martino Buon Albergo
SP10
Colognola
Sona
SR11
Verona Nord
SP1
6
8
Pieve
Soave
Palazzina
7
33 – 42
Verona Est
Vago
A 4
E 70
Sommacampagna
Caselle
Verona Sud
Caldiero
Zerbare
Sommacampagna
SP20
Castelletto
Fredda
Verona-Villafranca
Dossobuono
San Giovanni Lupatoto
Mambrotta
Belfiore
Ganfardine
Alpo
SP19
Zevio
SP26
SP25
Pontoncello
Monto del Quadrato
Dosdega
Ca' di David
Perzacco
Villafranca di Verona
A 22
Azzago
SP19
F. Adige
Castel d'Azzano
SS12
E
Piazza
Albaro
187

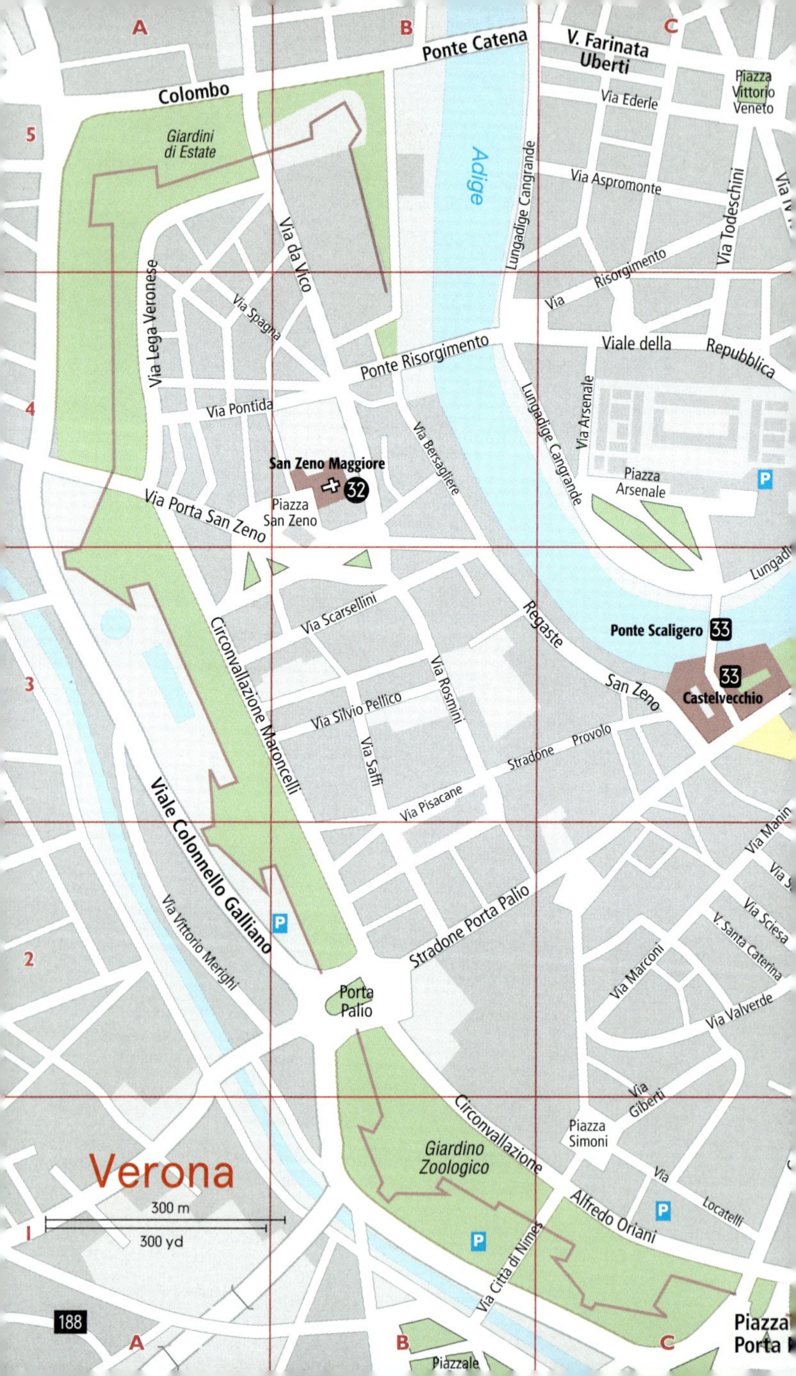

Verona
300 m
300 yd
A
B
C
5
4
3
2
1
Colombo
Ponte Catena
V. Farinata Uberti
Giardini di Estate
Via Ederle
Piazza Vittorio Veneto
Adige
Lungadige Cangrande
Via Aspromonte
Via Todeschini
Via da Vico
Via Lega Veronese
Via Spagna
Via Risorgimento
Viale della Repubblica
Ponte Risorgimento
Via Pontida
Via Arsenale
Lungadige Cangrande
Via Bersagliere
San Zeno Maggiore
32
Piazza Arsenale
Via Porta San Zeno
Piazza San Zeno
Lungadige
Via Scarsellini
Regaste San Zeno
Ponte Scaligero
33
Castelvecchio
Circonvallazione Maroncelli
Via Rosmini
Via Silvio Pellico
Via Saffi
Stradone Provolo
Via Pisacane
Viale Colonnello Galliano
Via Manin
Via Sciesa
V. Santa Caterina
Via Vittorio Merighi
Stradone Porta Palio
Via Marconi
Via Valverde
Porta Palio
Via Giberti
Piazza Simoni
Circonvallazione Alfredo Oriani
Giardino Zoologico
Via Locatelli
Via Città di Nimes
Piazza Porta
Piazzale

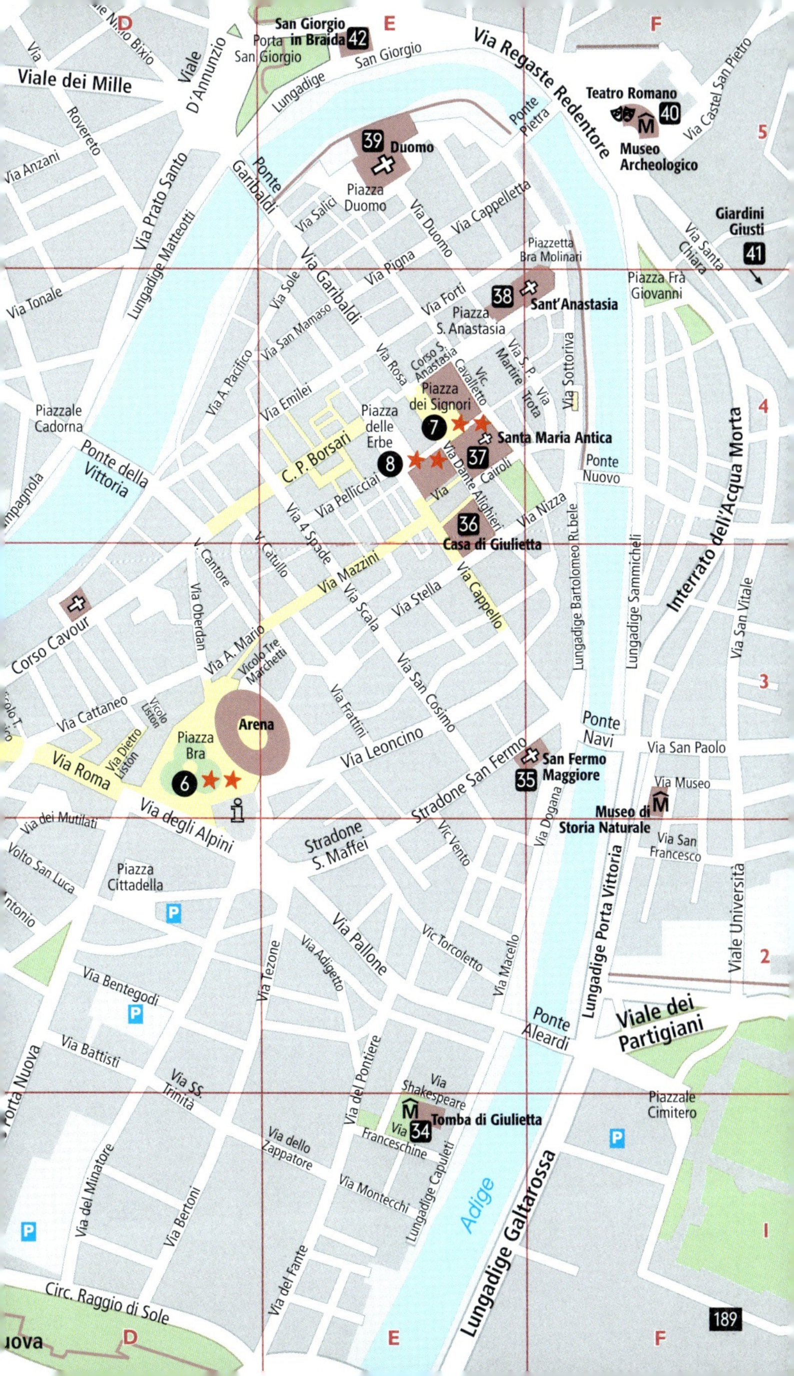

D
E
F
San Giorgio in Braida
42
Porta San Giorgio
San Giorgio
Lungadige
Via Regaste Redentore
Teatro Romano
40
Museo Archeologico
Via Castel San Pietro
5
Viale dei Mille
Viale D'Annunzio
Via Nino Bixio
Via Rovereto
Via Anzani
Via Prato Santo
Lungadige Matteotti
Ponte Garibaldi
39
Duomo
Piazza Duomo
Ponte Pietra
Via Salici
Via Duomo
Via Cappelletta
Piazzetta Bra Molinari
Giardini Giusti
41
Via Santa Chiara
Piazza Frà Giovanni
Via Tonale
Via Sole
Via Garibaldi
Via Pigna
Via Forti
38
Sant'Anastasia
Piazza S. Anastasia
Via San Mamaso
Via A. Pacifico
Via Emilei
Via Rosa
Corso S. Anastasia
Piazza dei Signori
Vic. Cavalletto
Via S. P. Martire
Via Trota
Via Sottoriva
4
Piazzale Cadorna
Piazza delle Erbe
7
Santa Maria Antica
Ponte Nuovo
8
37
C. P. Borsari
Via Pellicciai
Via Dante Alighieri
Via Cairoli
Ponte della Vittoria
Interrato dell'Acqua Morta
Via 4 Spade
Via Nizza
36
Casa di Giulietta
V. Cantore
V. Catullo
Via Mazzini
Via Oberdan
Via Scala
Via Stella
Via Cappello
Lungadige Bartolomeo Rubele
Lungadige Sammicheli
Via San Vitale
Corso Cavour
Via A. Mario
Vicolo Tre Marchetti
Via San Cosimo
3
Via Cattaneo
Vicolo Liston
Arena
Via Frattini
Ponte Navi
Via San Paolo
Piazza Bra
Via Dietro Liston
Via Roma
6
Via Leoncino
San Fermo Maggiore
35
Via Museo
Stradone San Fermo
Museo di Storia Naturale
Via dei Mutilati
Via degli Alpini
Via Dogana
Via San Francesco
Volto San Luca
Stradone S. Maffei
Vic. Vento
Piazza Cittadella
Lungadige Porta Vittoria
P
Via Pallone
Viale Università
Via Adigetto
Vic. Torcoletto
Via Macello
2
Via Bentegodi
Via Tezone
Ponte Aleardi
Viale dei Partigiani
Via Battisti
Via SS. Trinità
Via del Pontiere
Via Shakespeare
Piazzale Cimitero
Tomba di Giulietta
34
Via Franceschine
Porta Nuova
Via dello Zappatore
Via Montecchi
Lungadige Capuleti
Adige
Via del Minatore
Via Bertoni
Lungadige Galtarossa
1
Via del Fante
Circ. Raggio di Sole

Index

Picture Credits

AA/A. Mockford & N. Bonetti: p. 113, 164

age fotostock/Lookphotos: p. 19, 148

Toni Anzenberger: p. 5 top & bottom, 6 (8) & 111, 6 (10) & 140, 9, 10 bottom, 12/13, 15, 23 bottom left, 32, 40, 40/41, 48 bottom right, 53 top & bottom right, 57, 66/67, 71 top & middle, 72, 72/73, 78, 79, 88, 90, 91, 94, 101 top & middle, 103, 105, 114, 115, 117, 119, 131, 143, 144 top, 159, 162, 172/173

ClickAlps/Lookphotos: p. 139

DuMont Bildarchiv/Michael Riehle: p. 6 (1) & 43, 6 (3) & 80, 6 (5) & 85, 24, 26, 27, 39 top & bottom, 41, 42, 46, 48 bottom left, 51 bottom right, 53 bottom right, 54, 55, 56, 58, 60, 61, 62, 65, 71 &, 73, 77 top & bottom left/right, 81, 82, 87, 102/103, 152/153, 155, 163, 167

DuMont Bildarchiv/Sabine Lubenow: p. 6 (6) & 96/97, 25, 28, 29, 30, 102, 104, 121, 122

DuMont Bildarchiv/Thilo Weimar: p. 6 (7) & 109, 6 (9) & 133, 14, 17 top & bottom left/right, 31 top left & bottom left, 31 right, 33, 51 top, 64, 89, 101 &, 112, 129 left/right, 132, 134, 135 top & bottom left/right, 136, 144 bottom left/right, 146, 147 left/right, 151, 169 top & bottom left/right

Huber Images/Günter Gräfenhain: p. 141

Huber Images/Luca Da Ros: p. 6 (2) & 75

Huber Images/Luigi Vaccarella: p. 18

Huber Images/Massimo Ripani: p. 130 left

Huber Images/Matteo Carassale: p. 130 right

Huber Images/Stefano Scatà: p. 150

Huber Images/TC: p. 10 top, 23 top right, 34/35

laif/Tobias Gerber: 6 (4) & 47, 51 bottom left

LOOK-foto/TerraVista: p. 48 top

mauritius images/John Warburton-Lee: p. 108

On the Cover: Top: Tobias Gerber/laif
Bottom: Zahn/laif
Back: Tobias Gerber/laif

Credits

2nd Edition 2019
Fully revised and redesigned

Worldwide Distribution: Marco Polo Travel Publishing Ltd
Pinewood, Chineham Business Park
Crockford Lane, Chineham
Basingstoke, Hampshire RG24 8AL, United Kingdom.

Authors: Richard Sale, Frances Wolverton and Jochen Müssig
Editor: Robert Fischer (www.vrb-muenchen.de)
Revised editing and translation: Christopher Wynne
Design: CYCLUS · Visuelle Kommunikation, Stuttgart
Project manager: Dieter Luippold
Programme supervisor: Birgit Borowski
Chief editor: Rainer Eisenschmid

Cartography: © MAIRDUMONT GmbH & Co. KG, Ostfildern
3D illustrations: jangled nerves, Stuttgart

Printed in Poland

Despite all of our authors' thorough research, errors can creep in. The publishers do not accept any liability for this. Whether you want to praise us, alert us to errors or give us a personal tip – please don't hesitate to email or post:

MARCO POLO Travel Publishing Ltd
Pinewood, Chineham Business Park
Crockford Lane, Chineham
Basingstoke, Hampshire RG24 8AL
United Kingdom
Email: sales@marcopolouk.com

My Notes